Horace M. (Horace Mellard) Du Bose

Rupert Wise

A Poetic Romance In Eight Cantos

Horace M. (Horace Mellard) Du Bose

Rupert Wise
A Poetic Romance In Eight Cantos

ISBN/EAN: 9783744665445

Printed in Europe, USA, Canada, Australia, Japan

Cover: Foto ©Thomas Meinert / pixelio.de

More available books at **www.hansebooks.com**

RUPERT WISE:

A Poetic Romance.

IN EIGHT CANTOS.

By H. M. DuBose.

" Then, in a moment, she put forth the charm
Of woven paces and of weaving hands;
And in the hollow of the oak he lay as dead,
And lost to life and use and name and fame."

"I hold it truth with him who sings
To one clear harp in divers tones,
That men may rise on stepping-stones
Of their dead selves to higher things."
—*Baron Tennyson.*

PRINTED FOR THE AUTHOR.
PUBLISHING HOUSE OF THE METHODIST EPISCOPAL CHURCH, SOUTH.
J. D. BARBEE, AGENT, NASHVILLE, TENN.
1889.

PREFATORY.

"Poetry is itself a thing of God;
He made His prophets poets."

I KNOW not whether or not this message of mine be worthy the noble appellation of poetry. It rests with my countrymen to judge of its title to a place in the book of inspired song. But this I say, God taught it me. Ten years and more ago, amid humble labors in a village beside the Father of Waters, and when the shadow of the pestilence that walketh in darkness was but newly lifted from the hearts of a smitten people, my hand was first set to the task. The resonant voices of the onward tides taught me the numbers of a hitherto untried scale; a peaceful memory, brought from my childhood home in the pine-sentried hills, kept fresh in my soul the love of nature's reverberant melodies and her awful hushes of sacred melancholy; and the sad, sad story of unmerited bitterness that blighted a life more beautiful than "the fringed lilies" was the inspiration of this my lowly verse.   H. M. DuBose.

Los Angeles, Cal., October, 1889.

(3)

INTRODUCTION.

THE conscience of Christendom is becoming more and more sensible of the appalling evils that flow from the use of intoxicating liquors. Step by step, advancing in every legitimate path that is opened up, the enlightened judgment of the Christian world is taking a forward position, and demanding the rescue of fallen humanity from exposure to the unspeakable horrors of the drunkard's career.

Every contribution to this much-desired result is a subject of welcome and congratulation to society. Poets have sung the pleasures of the wine-cup; why should not the genius of the poet devote itself to the warning of the exposed and endangered, and to the reclamation of the enslaved? Can the inspiration of Parnassus be employed in a nobler service?

We have displayed in this poem, "Rupert Wise," the fearful truth that "no man liveth unto himself," even in respect to those things that are usually esteemed the chartered rights of personal liberty. Has any man the right to perpetuate, in his own offspring, the detestable vice of drunkenness? Has any man the right to acquire habits that may eventuate in the ruin of those who become the legatees of his errors and his crimes? The possibility of transmitting the taint of slavish bondage to the appetite for drink is the foundation of the argument in "Rupert Wise." This remorseless spell, weaving an enchantment too strong for earthly hopes, ambitions, or obligations to destroy, prepares the way for the darkness of the eternal night.

At the moment of despair, when the vision of female loveli-

(5)

ness, of earthly peace and quiet, love and joy, is about to die away in the fumes of the bottomless pit, the strong arm of the Redeemer of man reaches down to the verge of ruin, and snatches the brand from the eternal burning. The lesson is one that should sink deep into the heart of the reader. There is no vicious appetite that may not be conquered by the power of the grace of God manifested in Jesus Christ our Lord. "I can do all things through Christ which strengtheneth me." This truth forms the sequel.

The poem, as a work of art, is before the reader. The author makes his venture before the public unheralded by critics or by interested advocates, but if the "divine afflatus" of the true poet has fallen upon his spirit, and typed itself in this work of his pen, the candid judgment of the reader will indorse that of the editor of this volume. We believe that there is superior merit in this poem, and the promise of the higher work that is yet to be.   W. P. HARRISON.

Nashville, Tenn., October 18, 1889.

PROEMA.

WHEN early morn had lift its veil,
   Of woven mist from off a hill
   That all my sight with dreams did fill,
Half-way its slope, one calm and pale

I saw beneath the virgin shade.
   Strange garb was his, but noble all
   His bearing seemed. Swift at his call
I moved him near, and deference paid

To that mild air of worth he wore.
   Expectant wonder held my soul
   What time his hands unlaced a scroll,
That wizard trace of genius bore.

Wild joy I felt when that his name
   Was breathed—no other than the bard
   Who that Prince Arthur evil starred
Had sung to everlasting fame.

Brought forth from Alma's hidden scrine
   That antique roll of goodly knights
   Of Tanaquil, and those six lights
Of Faery Queen that ceased to shine.

" Swear on this scroll," he gravely said,
   "As sware Sir Guyon on his shield,
   By castle wall, in wood or field,
Fierce vengeance on the Paynim head,

"And that Acrasia, sorceress vile,
  Who Modrant and Amavia slew,
  Him with the cup's enchanted dew,
Her through despair and sorceress' wile.

"Acrasia lives with other name;
  Swear vengeance here, and move thou hence
  That others swear, withal, defense
Of faithful love and manhood's frame."

I sware, and heard his blessings spoke,
  And saw him fade, like mist, away,
  The whiles, with oaten pipe and lay,
Shepherds the infant day awoke.

CANTO FIRST.

I.

HARP of the Southland now! that sad hath slept
    Since that wild singer, 'neath the whispering leaves
That near the river dark their cadence wept,
    Awoke his last and plaintive song; whose sheaves
    Of truth and garlands, gleaned through morns and eves
Of sorrow filled with tread of coming death,
    He consecrated unto God—as heaves
The reedy bank to Autumn's earliest breath,
Awake, assist my song of love and vanquished death!

The soul that breathes this prayer thy mazes o'er
    Breathes likewise full its ardent wish abroad,
E'en to the utmost limit—line and shore—
    Of this predestined land, made one since strode
    In hate the form of war with dark inroad
Through sunny vales whose circles peace had hung
    With clamb'ring vines and graced with villas broad
And smiling fields, where late, when morn was young,
The reaper's harvest lay in rippling echoes rung.

Once more awake, though but to weep anew!
    That voice befits thy strings, befits whose hand

Would teach thy strings to throb hope's measures through.
  Ah, welladay! that voice befits the land·
That mourns her youngest, greatest bard; the band
That walked with him through fire to martial strains,
  And pallid hosts that kissed the brazen wand.
Quicken, my touch! take fire, my dull refrains!
O Southland harp, awake with wild, unwonted strains!

II.

Hail, city fair, throned on eternal hills,
  Hard by the mighty river's sullen flow!
Far o'er the morning's gilded mist, that fills
  With tow'r and dome and shimm'ring bow
  The wide expanse thy monarch seat below,
The weary helmsman hails thee with delight;
  Or mocks the gloom, if but thy beacons glow,
Conjuring oft with fancy's yearning sight
The cheerful glimm'rings of his own domestic light.

Nature's primeval work thy strength reveals;
  Where now thy marts, before Itasca rose,
Time's hoary form hath been and on thy hills
  Left his memorial; they knew repose
  While yon fair land felt aye the wreck and throes,
The ruin and the waste, of change, nor smiles
  Perennial now.   Full oft in rude embrace
The am'rous flood of virgin life despoils,
  Destroys each fond adornment of her face,
  With recompense of fleecy wealth and vintage place.

O'er nature's granite ramparts rise thy fanes,
    Pointing in prophecy the multitudes
That move with listless mien along thy lanes
    To man's last end; or when the storm-king broods
    In ether's deep and vaulted solitudes,
Or rears his form upon the lightning's path
    And thunder th' elemental strife preludes,
Invite his bolts and kiss away his wrath;
For chaos knows his realm and ruin knows his path.

Red war around thy gates hath flamed, and Mars
    Hath looked with eyes of fiery curse on thee,
While fates malign and tracts of evil stars
    Have marked with lurid fears thy destiny;
    Yet queenly still thou sittest, clothed and free;
The past thou hast in tears, the future's page
    Thou holdest fair for peaceful history;
Though writ with golden pen for golden age,
Thou still wilt hold thy past, with good or ill presage.

To thee relates my song of various key;
    To thee pertains my tale, in thee 'twas wrought.
I own from thee the sense of mystery,
    And power of strong desire, in youth begot;
    To thee anon turns mem'ry ever fraught
With old-time visions of that free, grand tide,
    Moving majestic tow'rd its ocean lot,
Life symboling through all its glinting pride;
And thy green hills around, though winter all beside.

Thine are these garlands, gathered most where wave
  The dark-tressed willow-trees, and lowly blow
The daffodils on beauty's early grave;
  From darksome ways the tow'ring cliffs below,
  Where those red foils, sad bleeding-hearts, do grow,
Admixed with thorn-set sprays of eglantine
  And nightshade blooms, that fringèd petals show .
Through sun-scorched links of resurrection vine,
Whose germs revive from mold—these, mother, these are
    thine!

III.

Well through his northern signs bold Phœbus pressed,
Now quitted slowly Virgo's starry breast;
And Sirius, with dread, unequal sphere,
Leading the Sothian train through wide career,
Stood in the Archer's wake till, far and dim,
He shone serene on evening's azure rim;
But ere his exit into nether space
Red blazed awhile his ill-portending face;
Which dire menace, explained by thoughtful wight,
Spread terror round and din of wild affright;
Nor this alone bespoke impending ire:
The planet train in aug'ry dark conspire
And held their poisèd spheres on evil plane,
What time the comet shook his deadly mane
O'er pleasant lands, and deep resounding far
Came tokens of the earthquake's hidden war.

But mundane nature else reflected wide
The pangless scenes of Eden's nascent pride,

And mocked with piping sounds in sylvan void
Each rankling sense that hapless man annoyed;
Calm slept the fields where fruitful summer dreamed;
Full through the vales a wealth of sunlight streamed;
A Sabbath peace the distant spaces filled,
Where zephyr's hand along the forest trilled
With sounds that spoke Almighty presence nigh;
And latticed paths, besprint with crimson dye,
Led toward the sunset city's burnished gate,
Where fancy walks and dreams aspiring wait.

Sad contrast held in that fair city's life,
Besmit but late of war and wasting strife,
Yet since renewed in every peaceful thought
And, in a progress blood and sorrow bought,
Vying with compeers raised by fortune's hand
To higher state, the urbarchs of the land.
No more, alas! breathed hope where her tall spires,
Aglow with sunset's wide reflected fires,
O'erlooked a thousand homes to shame unknown,
A thousand hearths where humble virtue shone,
And in the unseen censers of the heart
The priestess Love her incense burned apart.
Now apprehension's dread Nemesis walked
Through erstwhile joyful scenes, and brooding stalked
Through crowded ways or cast in busy marts
A haunting shade. Compelled by terror's arts,
The rabble blanched at folly's idle tale,
And nobler senses owned the subtle bale;

A hidden scepter swayed the fateful hour
As fear succeeding fear renewed its power,
Nor wisdom's word, nor science' just disdain
Availed to check the passions' frenzied reign.

Convened apart by mutual sanction late,
As oft their wont, for pleasure and debate,
The wise physicians of the town appear
In council free to soothe a rising fear
By rumor of a distant scourge inspired,
And name such action as the case required.

Assembled once, the healing brotherhood
With grave demean and words their task pursued.
Though hope and wisdom speak of fate amiss
And seem o'erwhelmed, they know the abyss
And smile the darkness through to walk at last
In fairer ways, to nobler fashion cast.
Whom first the argument of hope to state,
O verse, affirm, and wisdom celebrate!
Of form commanding and imposing mien,
An air of leisure and a brow serene,
Past middle years yet youth's inspiring light
Still kindled in his eye of keenest sight
And spoke the ready grace of cultured speech
And skill that knew his fav'rite lore to teach.
Now flashed his eye as fervidly he said:
"My faith abides that danger hence is fled;
Sure breaks apace the season's deadly spell
And hope e'en now persuades that all is well.

Our teaching brooks not seer nor fabler's lore,
We draw our wiser proofs from safer store;
Yet, if the countless oracles without
Spoke forth, they name no moiety of doubt;
There is no taint upon the moving air;
The skies are mild, nor evil tokens bear;
Soft dews renew the chalice of the night
And spread elixir through the welcome light;
Nor voice, nor sign the fever plague invites,
But each, when told, an ardent hope excites
Of long immunity from evil state.
Our house in order stands for adverse fate;
As ne'er before we wait the scourge prepared;
To famed resorts our affluent ones are fared,
While others, lured by peace devoid of pride,
In rural cots and neighboring seats abide.
To vainly boast is scarce removed from crime,
Yet, if I rightly calculate the time,
'Tis five years since his saffron face we saw,
When science, hand in hand with social law,
Challenged his savage and unbridled reign
As foreign foe the nation might restrain.
Henceforth at ocean's verge the curse must stay,
Nor dare renew by stealth his former sway.
All this—who doubts?—is earnest of the day
When man, progressed to high and favored state,
With dark intrigues and mad decrees of fate
And such misfortune as belongs to chance,
Shall measure equal strength, and thus enhance

The glory of his days and raze withal
The frowning mass of fate's opposing wall.
For that fair goal the general purpose pants
And thrills expectant at the next advance!"

As silent touch of twilight's dewy spell
Falls o'er and stills the rustling wood, so fell
This cheerful speech the learnèd circle on,
Approved of all, save one, observant grown
From long experience in the plague-cursed climes
Of tropic lands.   High wish in other times,
When youth was strong and science held
Commanding sway of thought, had hence impelled
To brave insidious death and in his lair
Attack that dread whose coming brought despair.

He, rising, statue poised a moment stood,
His face betraying old Acadian blood;
Then bent his comely form in conscious pride,
And to his brother's ardent words replied:
"Your reasoning as it runs is fair to hear,
And if not sound at least will please the ear;
'Twere pleasant task such logic to imbibe
And to your transcendental creed subscribe;
But vain I fear your prophecy of good.
Alas, if time should blight this cheerful mood,
And leave where hopes rejoice but fortitude!
The fever rages now in all Balize;
Cuba is not without the fell disease;
And Key West, though the truth is hard to gain,
I much suspect has kept her isle in vain;

And mem'ry serves me of a time long gone—
My home was in the ancient Creole town—
The ending of a season much like this;
The summer waned, and nothing went amiss;
September's sultry days were growing mild;
The evenings dropped like visions undefiled;
The natives dreamed, as thousands from the States,
No evil nigh, when suddenly the fates
Seemed all their iron hands to lift and wage
Relentless war alike on youth and age.
As bands of armèd men that long had lain
In stealthy wait, the fever rose amain,
And heaped the city in a day with slain.
Full fierce it broke, full fierce from fifty points,
Yet, strange to tell, that year the rule disjoints:
No fever could be traced on all the seas,
In tropic lands no tidings of the dread disease,
And we alone of all the world were cursed.
We deal with fierce and stealthy foe, nor durst,
If still our wits abide, a respite take
Till winter's winds our benison shall make."

To this a third returned in tones of mirth,
Although half moved to own the reason's worth:
  "You then would have us write and seal our wills,
Our epitaphs inscribe, since shuffling haste
  Is like to leave no time therefor. But ills
There be of greater moment than this last.
  A prudent care is worthy noblest wills;
But man by fear unnerved is man debased."

Pasteur, for such the mild Acadian's name
(With him, as else, not all unknown to fame),
Thus made reply : " I speak a danger near,
An apprehension nowise born of fear,
But of that better mind which warns and cheers ;
Yet, though 'tis so, no remedy appears,
We stand an inland port, nor say nor choose
What tonnage we will pass, or what refuse.
Our Congress should this vital matter meet,
And give our subtle foe a last defeat.
The war must open at the nation's door,
And press this dragon to the ocean's shore ;
Ay, more than this, in sooth, must then befall:
Each lurking-place, each haunt by city's wall,
Each reeking vault where death resides,
His ally proves ; a thousand gates besides
Are open in the viewless air, nor doubt,
A cause is found within as found without—
These, too, must know the conquering war ; must prove
The strength of truceless law, ere forward move
Our people's hopes.   As men who own the sense
Of public trust, the present's dire suspense
We must with active counsel meet.   A plea
I recommend to every house to see
Its part in shaping of the city's good
By strict regard to health in air and food.
Should all to this without dissent agree,
I trust me much no plague's advent to see."

By tact of skill and drift of various mind,
To jousts of wit the wordy war inclined.
The council heard, a moment now concerned,
Now moved to action, now to lightness turned,
And having met by sage advice the call,
In social trend the learnèd gossips fall.
"Let's to the weed," one cries, "why cheat
Ourselves of this? for little seems it meet
To give to life alone of solemn care,
When hangs its changing fortunes, bad and fair,
On such capricious chance!"

                  With no dissent,
The fragrant weed around the circle went.
Thus passed an hour in pleasant sort beguiled,
Like bivouac scenes, where thoughts of carnage wild,
Though lurks he near with gory hands and feet,
Enter no more than into love's retreat,
Till he whose proud Acadian features burned
With anxious thought the discourse mildly turned:

"Now pardon grant, if I disposed should seem
Too much to chase an interdicted theme;
'Tis social matter that I would unfold
Which grows in wonder as the tale is told.
You each, no doubt, have marked the rapid rise,
The wealth and growing fame of Rupert Wise,
Our young Hippocrates who two years since,
From lectures fresh, took up his residence
In modest style on Celis Parlor Heights;
The case is rare, and me it much delights.

From first, he showed unusual skill and tact;
His birth, his high-born ways but touched the fact;
Puzzled, I sought for reasons more exact,
But wonder late is shorn of sense and word;
By this day's post I have the latest *Record.*
It bears young Rupert's autograph descant,
'*The germs of fever shown to be a plant,*'
Replete with learning's force, in logic strong,
Quite bold enough for learnèd dean, *savant,*
Or titled master of the healing art;
Indeed, I style the same a master-part.
'Tis freely said (the *Record* gave the hint,
Seconded by a leading Eastern print)
This treatise wins its author recognition
And 't may be, in time, a decoration;
'Twere but a step across the water then;
A twelvemonth more, perchance, with famous men,
Though overleaping precedents and rules,
Our colleague may be named in Old World schools."

Now spake the senior of the brotherhood,
A man benign, who seemed in youth renewed
At threescore years, as if of Heaven's will
Some high estate to grace or aptly fill
Some lot requiring ripest thought.   To him
Fortune was not the gross return or whim
Of fickle chance, but mind untarnished, clear,
With large support of soul to soothe and cheer
The mind through arduous tasks.   Him they hear:

"A lively interest rises in my breast
For this same youth, and 'tis to be confessed
As no mean cause for sense of pride to us
And to our calling that he prospers thus;
His parts and words show genius' fair impress;
His birth and station speak; nor less express
His comely modesty and easy bearing—
A dress admired, but one of rarest wearing—
Like any Greek, young Rupert wears his grace;
Adonis scarce possessed more handsome face.
These well might win him foremost rank and place,
But grounds exist for doubt and friendly fear,
Indeed, what soon must reach the public ear
'Tis safe to iterate in private way;
Although in mind and frame and social stay,
In noble plans, he firm and anchored seems,
One darkest curse dims all his future dreams,
And one which, though we understand too well,
Binds oft our brotherhood with cruel spell,
This same hath set on him its base impress—
He loves the cup and drinks to mad excess."

Hereat a third caught up the growing tale—
A bachelor of prim attire, with pale
And smirking face; a gallant in his day,
But now grown stern, with but the feeblest ray
Of tender light left in his eyes of blue:
"Not current goes the story, yet quite true;
This Rupert has a love affair: therein
The secret of his life and of his sin

Grows deep in coloring : its heroine
A fair and fragile girl, one Madeline,
A planter's child, petted, adored, and sought,
Yet, strange to say, not spoiled, displaying naught
In wish or act but speaks uncommon mind.
Most to such converse seems her thought inclined
As touches noble action, conquers doubt,
And calls the subtlest points of logic out;
Withal a child and artless as the wind,
Veering to trivial sense of womankind:
A kirtled queen, Minerva sewing floss,
'Twixt stellar problems smoothing birdie's gloss.
She loves young Wise, nor other passion knew.
From early childhood side by side they grew,
But this one vice has cleft them far apart;
Her hand she keeps, yet gives him all her heart.
His bold agnosticism, cold and flippant doubt,
He hides from her, whose soul is most devout
And, true to woman's faith, bids love remain
Till love itself shall heal her every pain.
She lives a tearful hope that soon or late
His manhood may assert itself, and fate
Be changed to happier current in the end ;
And so her thought preserves a peaceful trend.
But hope, alas! is vain.   He who can hold
His treason out against such love is sold
To baseness and an evil self—a slave
To appetite—and merits not to have
One kindly thought, far less such love as this !
Hope there is not this side the grave's abyss,

This side of Hades or the waves of Styx,
Or such dread state as guilty fear depicts,
That he will cease to quaff the fiery shame,
Though maiden's blood mixed with its liquid flame.
His father, rich and strong and fitted well
For honors high in state, and born to tell
The rights of man, who even in tender youth
Was forward in such things and loved the truth,
Later the friend of Prentiss and to him
Second alone in flexive speech, less dim
In thought, and bolder in all argument—
Alas, too much like him in evil bent!
He quenched (sad fate!) in wine that god-like fire
And died bereft of mind, as beasts expire!
How can we better of the son, who sprung
From stem diseased, self-nurtured and so young,
Reveals the vice as genius of his sire?"

Pasteur, the darker shades of thought that lay
Along his mind, like clouds upon the day,
Chased by the sun of merriment away,
Twitted these earnest words with hidden jest:
"You speak with warmth; in reason one had guessed
You look yourself with passion's eye that way.
Too long you've left that matter of the heart
To want; too long withstood the tender art;
You late confessed to six and fifty years,
'Tis not a sound to please a maiden's ears,
So now repress your passion's rising force
And settle down to pills and dry discourse."

The answer came as from a long-forbidden source:
" Too fair and pure a realm is woman's love,
Too sacred all its heavenly visions prove,
For soul like mine.   Afar I gaze, admire,
But know no thoughts so mad as thence aspire;
Her worth I own, confessed in earlier days,
Nor deem a fault the affluence of my praise.
In sooth, for this fair maid I feel concern,
Though only such as lighter thoughts might turn;
For, truth to tell, acquaintance ne'er so slight
I boast with Madeline; a stiff, polite,
And hasty introduction on the guards,
A friendly salutation afterwards,
Tell all our intercourse from first to last,
Nor shade of tender thought its memories cast."

" Your words," Pasteur replied, " echo romance:
' Upon the guards '—a trivial circumstance,
Yet many life arrangements owe their force
To no more serious thing—an easy course,
A salutation here or there by chance,
A glint of moonlight through the night's expanse,
Mutual tastes discovered, friendly ways,
An idyl through the sloth of summer days,
A walk, a drive, and trysts on quiet eves,
A pledge, a vow, the fall of autumn leaves,
A dash of winter winds, a burst of light
Through perfumed halls, the golden circlet's plight,
A wedding chant, the lapse of life's content,
A quiet home—and so the thread of life is spent."

"Avaunt! for shame! to tickle ears like mine
With words that speak such gushing thought! New wine
Meets not the old, nor can you graft the rose
Upon the hawthorn bough; its forms oppose
The ruder fiber of the weathered tree,
So dreams of maids and love befit not me.
Go, put your ravings in a penny book,
And then, perchance, some maiden, love forsook,
Some idle dreamer under summer's sky
Will read, and you more wealth shall gain thereby
Than you are like to see the whole year through
By magic of your skill and nostrums too."

To end this witty tilt, broke in once more
The senior's voice; not listless as before
His air, but changed and heavy was his mood
With fears augmented and the gath'ring load
Of danger felt.   Thus spake he, blending well
A tinge of mirth with sadder words that fell:
" Enough! enough! break off, your speeches tire;
They tell a task essayed without desire
And mind me of a scene that marked the days
When iron monsters fringed with lurid blaze
The river's strand before the city's front,
And through the dragging weeks we felt the brunt
Of leaden war.   The lines of bristling steel
Fell like a wall across the land; to feel
The pinch of want became our daily mood,
For nothing came, and direr grew the need.

'Twas on that last eventful day I stood
Before the baker's door in speechless mood.
He seemed to read my fear nor left a doubt,
But answered straight: 'My friend, the dough is out!'
But whence his thought or what his words' import
'Twere bootless now to ask.   Instant report
Confirmed the town's surrender to the foe.
Whether 'twere that or lack of cakes and dough
I did not further seek.   In either place
The rule applies, so rest this fruitless case.
The hours have far tow'rd somber midnight waxed,
Your honored heads for wit are overtaxed;
To-morrow's sun will bring to each, I ween,
New toils; but hours of slumber intervene,
And well behooves it us to seek repose;
The fear we fain would scorn more real grows.
A fortnight's space our hopes will make or mar;
But, come what may, we're entered for the war."

Now midnight clothed in shades and ebon gloom
The favored town, and silence as of doom
Held cot and lofty dome in mute embrace;
The watch-stars, mounting toward their vigil place,
In shining ranks approached the sable tower,
And flung their beams creation's vastness o'er.
What darkness looked they on! what sorrow read
Through latticed ways, where smothered dread
Spoke forth in sleepless eyes or forced its seal
On fevered lips and brows too soon to feel
The fiercer touch of mortal ill!

While yet
The darkness held its sway and cold dews wet
His thick, neglected locks, the night patrol—
A stern, unflinching man, who softly stole
Like some dark specter, year by year, along
The silent streets and alleys dark among—
Anon heard phantom feet upon the wind
While viewless horsemen trode the night behind,
And cried the van-guard of a coming woe,
Hurried themselves from peaceful scenes below
To that far bourne with dread and evil haste.
Others protest a tall fierce spirit paced
From cottage door to marble balcony
And marked with strange device each casement high—
Some say with shape like demon's cloven hoof,
Others with sign of such attenuate proof
As spirit sight alone avails to read—
Earnest of course the besom death should lead.

The sexton, old and full of monkish dote,
Related how a sacred hand had smote
In sleep that night his withered form, and led
Him forth where slept inurned the mold'ring dead,
And planned him twoscore hundred open graves,
Blessing with chalice and the prayer that saves,
So that the unshriven dead might rest at least
In holy ground while death pursued his feast.
Protesting still with fear and reverend faith,
The ancient man recalled his father's wraith

Ofttimes had filled his sight, when that his death
The circling months had brought to mind; his breath
Returned to warn some evil must befall
His offspring near that fatal day; withal
That night his father's ghost in deep concern
Appeared, and from its legendary urn
In Tara old, o'er ocean forced to fly,
His family banshee lifted mortal cry;
He, hapless man, the last of that high trust,
The banshee hence must sleep with Tara's dust!

CANTO SECOND

I.

WHO nameth life? The deep portentous gloom
That drops anon when breaks its borrowed spell;
The silent gleam of stars from morning's womb;
    The sudden burst of daylight's conqu'ring swell;
    The bounding into sunlit ways, where dwell
The living thoughts of shape and mold divine
    That speak of wise and tender wish and tell
Some kindred hand, impelled by love's design,
    Hath spread its palm, in kingly wise, to bless;
    And voice that bids the night be day, nor welcome less.

Who nameth life? A dream, a fading cloud—
    Fantastic wanderer of a boundless sky,
Gilded with unenduring light, or plowed
    By angry storms. Unchosen choice! we cry
    For length of days and drink the chalice dry,
Supposing this were all. Mystery dread!
    Yet sweet because so much a mystery;
Joy born of pain and life born of the dead:
    And clouds that travail with the thunder's pain
    Weep liquid life and sweetness on the fruitful plain.

II.

Hard by a wide expanse of inland waves,
Where primal warmth of summer's sunshine laves
The fruitful acres of an old demesne,
A lordly homestead rises up between
A vistaed range of Lombard boles that stand,
Like domeless columns in a wasted land.
Green darkness, cast by elms and ancient limes,
Half hides the lofty gables, porch, and rimes
Of weathered stucco under Scottish tiles
That glisten white and red above the leafy aisles.
Northward the boundless furrowed valleys range,
Alternate white and brown with staples' change;
Southward the verdant pasture lands outroll
To marge on sinuous glade and amber pool,
Lavish of grassy fens and cockle dells,
Rifled by soft-eyed kine to sound of tinkling bells.

Here dwelt, in exile from the world's desire,
That Madeline who cheered her widowed sire
With reverent speech and love's adjusted power,
Beguiling evening's still and dusky hour
With gentlest service, duteous constancy,
With lute and lay of pleasing minstrelsy,
Yet nursed within her bosom's spotless scrine
The cruel pang that passing years refine—
The pang of hope deferred, of love unwise—
An angel fearing its own paradise.
The wine of joy from bitter lees was bred,
And cheerful words, like leaves of roses wed

To thorny stem, sat on a heart that bore
Such poignant grief as pierced it to its inmost core

Now came the eve, such eves as bless
This favored land: roseate flush and stress
Of sunset skies and soft south winds that shake
Ambrosial sweetness from the flow'ry brake,
And mild intoxicants of odorous breaths
From clustered elder-boughs and bulbous wreaths
Of great magnolia-trees; murmurous sounds
Of nature's mingling under-tones, and rounds
Of far-off notes some dusky troubadour
Chants lustily alone, his labors o'er;
Or distant throbbings of the heart of steam
In some grim packet's side, riding the stream
With fleecy freight—its deep and muffled swells
Prophetic of the plaint that fate compels
From heart of universal man, who stems
The tide, distraught of weight that peace condemns.
Monitions, too, of spirit essence move
Upon the soul, and every power involve
In quick gestations of delightful sense.
Such eve prevailed, and 'neath the soft defense
Of clamb'ring vines that trailed her garden o'er
Walked Madeline with anxious thought and sore,
Caressing as she passed each floret's head,
And on each petal lip a trembling tear-drop shed.

O guerdon pure of our lost Eden bliss!
Sweet recompense of grief and hope amiss!

The flowers that wilding blush in woodland shade,
Or blow beside the hedge or, beauty rayed,
Grace garnered fields and home's love-lighted bowers—
God's love be praised for love and leaves and flowers!
"Behold, into my garden I am come!"
The Rose of Sharon saith, the sweet Bridegroom.
Was it the vale of tears, Gethsemane,
Death gloomed from rugged brow of Calvary,
Where, with torn hands and anguish-riven heart,
He plucked rich spicery boughs and myrrh, a part
Of His own self, that tree of life that grew
Hard by the fontal wave, under the seventh blue?
O lily! one red spot thy whiteness shows;
I kiss thy petals, and the wonder grows,
For in thy deepest heart it crimsons most.
Not one sweet drop of that rich blood was lost.
Heldest thou forth a chalice pure as love
To drink? Irreverent must thou seem to prove,
O anxious faith? Howbeit, this I know,
He loved the flowers, and ever told his woe
To them, and breathed on them his tend'rest breath,
Making them tell the tale of life and death
As seen through his mild eyes, and chose his hour
When flow'ring Nisan dropped its shower
Of asphodels and wild thyme everywhere,
And when he slept at last they laid him there,
In Joseph's garden where the fringèd lilies were.
Eftsoon a weeping Magdalene found,
Lingering still that sacred vault around,

In whom she read the simple gardener's mien
Till that his voice revealed the Nazarene.
Might Madeline, the broken-hearted, find
Amongst her flowers that same "Rabboni" kind!

The summer winds toyed with her flowing hair,
Exotics rained their perfumes on the air,
And cast a wealth of waxen forms that grew
More sweet when crushed beneath her dainty shoe.
A broken urn lay near, its dead anemones
Typing too well love's wasted memories.
Her fragile fingers clutched a penciled sheet,
Its dainty seal and tinted covering neat
That, dropped by chance, lay on a bed of phlox,
Like alabaster set in crusted blocks
Of purple gems above a temple's shrine,
Bespeaking tracery of words divine,
Whose sense must needs have smit with fatal force
A heart already quenched at vital source.
Her dark-brown eyes that lustrous shone were fair
With frenzying light, but mute despair
　　Had settled on the face of perfect mold
That showed insensate whiteness like the sheen
Of some pale star through vapory moonlight seen;
　　And now the dark eyes' light grew pensive, cold,
The quiv'ring lips in troubled accents moved,
And breathed a speech that erst too much had proved:

"Courage, my woman's heart, be brave and stout,
Though sorrow lade and passion measure out
Each crimson drop that warmly courses thee,

And leave with each a grief its own to be,
Though thou hast felt of hope the utmost pain
Till, suffering long, thou knewest hope was vain;
Though thou hast felt the torturing sense and smart
Of newborn shame and fate's relentless art—
Nathless, my tear-scorched heart, I bid be still,
Of bitter tears thou canst but weep thy fill!

"'Woman, why weepest thou?' a tender voice
Asked long ago. Weeping is not thy choice,
But aye has been thy lot: a wild swept harp
Since first that heart was bared to feel the sharp,
Fierce blasts without those sun-blest vales that made
Its earliest home. That thou hast dearly paid
Thy fault, let say old tales of sword and lust
From leagured towns; and desert-withered dust
Of ancient capitals; let her that wept
Beside the Ilian distaff, they that kept
Campana's furrowed fields bedewed with tears,
And Punic daughters, from their birth to curse
Of foreign shame foredoomed, and Attic maids,
And that long line of weeded mourning shades
That moves through history's dim-aisled, mystic fane,
Attest with soul-born throes of undeservèd pain!
These filled their tearful lots and went their way,
Fading at autumn touch of sorrow's day,
To spring again by some still vernal wave
Beyond the hazy doubts that skirt the grave,
No withering leaf of hope to know, no sigh
Of blasting winds—they waited, suffering; so must I.

"If love essays, as oft in other days,
    To cast its horoscope of joyful wish,
And sweeps along the future's veilèd years,
    But swift, portentous shadows darkly rush,
Like evil things, before my troubled gaze,
    And ne'er a favoring star or sign appears.
I cannot trust that fond delusive thought
    That strengthened ties and scalèd bridal vows
Will break an evil pow'r, more evil fraught,
    That love restrained and hope deferred break not;
    To yield to fate that last restraint endows
With evil absolute a now thrice bitter lot.

"But once again, yet once again; perchance, I slight
    Some word, some simple, doubly precious word
That, like a window tow'rd the dawning light,
    Lets morning through with touch of hallowed peace.
    O lines by true love tears already blurred,
    And waking fateful echoes that shall cease
Only when soul shall stand to soul revealed
    In that consuming Presence, knowing all,
Give forth thy secret, if there be concealed
    In thee one gleam of hope or duty's higher call!"

The tearful eyes once more review the written sheet
Whose passioned words the evening winds repeat:
    "Sweet Madeline, hear this my latest plea
So often made 'tis moved by dolorous sighs;
    Now writ in tears and well-nigh scaled with blood.
    In prison dark, my soul goes out to thee,

Lifts up its voice, and fondly, wildly cries
　　For help from thy dear hands. A rising flood
　Of fears and doubts o'erwhelm, but in the full
Abiding strength of that deep love of thine
I seek repose. 'Tis thou, of earthly or divine,
　　Hast pow'r to soothe my troubled thoughts and lull
The angry storm and wasting strife within.
　　Pity, if thou canst pity one so weak,
And quickly come, thou radiant dream of love,
　　Thou morn of peace, into my life and speak
　　The gracious word that seals thee ever mine
And seals me unto honor's self and prove
　　That power which daily I extol as thine;
Bid me attend thy will, and lo! I come
Swift as the mated doves that seek their home
　　When sudden storms burst on their aerie flight.
　　'Tis honor bids me say I still am bound;
　But thou, my angel keeper, thou hast might,
When nuptial love shall ripen in its time,
　　To break each ling'ring fetter and proclaim
　　　Me free. Heal thou my soul's corroding wound;
　Bid me return, as erst, in thy sweet name!
My days are exile; long I for that clime
　In which my boyhood's heart felt glad surprise
　And drank thy smiles. Forever, Rupert Wise."

"Nay, never can it be, although each flow'r
　That blossomed fresh in girlhood's peaceful morn
Be blighted by the word, and envious dust
　Rest on their petals, and each rapture born

With them be turned to grief, and though the rust
　　Dim all my altar gold, it may not be.
Thou seest, soul, the path grows many a thorn,
　　But thou shalt tread it since 'twas made for thee.
Decide I must; be this the moment and the hour.
　　O that I had a friend on whom to lean!
Some kindred heart to share my heavy load,
　　That walking, in my somber world, between
Their love and His who shed his kingly blood
　　To give me final peace, I might find strength
　　To journey on through all life's weary length!
O for the voice of her who gave me birth!
　　O for a mother's constant thought to lead
The way!　But long the cold obstructive earth
　　Has claimed that gentlest friend.　They laid her head
On lowly pillow in the vale where oft I trod
　　In childhood's years, undreaming of my loss,
Undreaming of this hour, hid save from God,
　　Undreaming of the fate that soon should toss
The life that she so fondly prayed might know
　　But peaceful days and fruited joys on seas
Thrice turbulent with breaking waves, and show
　　Of envious chance that on misfortune preys.
O mother, does thy waking spirit hear
　　My prayers, the burdening sighs I heave,
Or know when I am near thy lonely grave?
　　Say, mother, does thy soul regard thy child
When on that grave she drops the pensive tear,
　　And mourns thy life's sweet scope and vision o'er?

O canst thou through this evening twilight mild
  Look down—ay, dost thou see me evermore?
I am a pilgrim in the way, beguiled
  No more by earth, and soon shall be as thou.
Oft when I bow at evening time for prayer,
  I feel unearthly impress on my brow,
As if some guardian spirit's touch were there;
  O tell me, mother, is that impress thine?
Enough! I know that thou art near me here;
  Thy life of love, thy memory's constant bloom,
Breathe patient trust. The higher will is mine!
  Yon fair ascending star whose beams are shed
In radiance half melodious round thy tomb
  A beacon light becomes, and safe shall lead
My trustful spirit heavenward, sunward, home!'

As swells the rising sea with refluent shock,
When back recoiling from the buttressed rock,
So rose the maiden's soul upon the wave
Of troubled sense that into silence drave
And seemed to die, but backward turned and wrought
With misty hands a spectral dread in thought.
Long time she stood, with strong decision spent
In one concern, and thus her purpose went:

"My father wills it, and I make my own
  That kind paternal thought, with kindred near.
In that dear Old Dominion clime, now grown
  More dear, to bide the fading of the year;

To those fair mountains lifting their blue heads
    Above the scenes of beauty in the vale
Where, like a tender wilding flower that spreads
    Its petals to the wooing breezes, frail
As their induing breath, my mother grew
    To blissful maidenhood, I turn with hope;
There still, perhaps, with sweetness like the dew
    That lingers in the lily's nodding cup
When down the night withdraws the bridegroom sun,
    Her spirit, virgin robed, abides my prayer.
There will I seek repose, if e'er that boon
    For my torn heart kind Heaven on earth prepare,
Or else I shall find rest, unbroken rest,
    In silent sleep beside the gliding wave,
While o'er my head the spring doves coo and nest
    And blue-eyed clovers weep above my grave.

" Who knows that unrevealèd life beyond?
    Enough that in the bosom of its years
Love shall not bring despair, nor vital bond
    Be loosed with rain between of fruitless tears!
Ay, Heaven is kind! perchance I there shall know
    His faultless love, and winds of paradise
Shall catch from bowers that dust untarnished blow
    The old-time vows, breathed ere that thralling vice
Had walked within the shadow of our faith.
    O Father, must thy noblest work, despoiled
And marred, be left to shame eterne? Why saith
    Thy word ' His angels shall have charge, lest toiled
Of sin he dash his foot the stones against?'

Shall guardian spirits arch in vain their wings
Above that laureled head?   Must that bold light
   Of goodly intellect that flows like springs
Of infant day go out in deepest night?
   Nay! saith a wish that will not be denied,
A wish that by thy certain promise plain'st:
   Must mercy, moved to die, in vain have died?
Yet will I trust and hold thy promise true;
   Our weakness is thy might, and still thou deign'st
Our prayers and cries, nor dost thy pleasure rue.
   I will believe thee better than our fears,
Ay, better than our highest faith hath made,
   Or even our tenderest speech can frame
A thought of thee!   Whether from sorrow laid,
   Or bliss breathed, on our hearts there wake the flame
Of purer joys and nobler wish, appears
   To feeble sight the mask of cruel chance;
But who loves not the weeping harp-string best,
   And who feels not his soul rise on the trance
Of plaintive song?
                    "Alas! I am unblest
   With holy memory of a love whose glance
Were like some kindly star's, ascendant proved
   At natal hour and holding forth through life
A potent charm.   Yet to my fate I loved,
   And that deep thought was in my being rife,
And wrought into the texture of my soul.
   So long ago my tender mind retained
No memory of the day, love on the scroll,
   The fair and hidden scroll, of life detained

His fiery wand and wrote one only name.

Dream not, ye winds, I love no more.   That fire
Shall burn with inextinguishable flame,
    As vestal altar on, lighting the pyre
Of every earthly hope, as one by one
    The days consign them to their doom.   Yet so
We meet, redeemed at last from evil done,
    And purged from dross, what matter now I know
Such fiery test? what though my spirit cry?
    It shall be well.   With that dear hope how short
The years to wait; yet doubts, that say not why,
    Are mine; nor more is made of winds the sport
Yon shredded gossamers that toss on high
    Than I the sport of fear and soul's misgivings.
Why must we suffer so and lift a fruitless cry
    Who are the crown of life and first of things?
The swallow circling toward the brim
    Of yonder sun-dyed wave knows joy alone,
And love at evening's close will answer him
    From out the nest beside the chimney stone;
Ah, should our summer tide at last begin,
    Through circling of the endless years above,
And we, its sunny bosom resting in,
    But hear the purer accents of our love,
Chased by the winter of unrest from earth,
    It will be well.   O God, thou know'st to prove
Our love; in death, to give it better birth!"

With dusky wings the shadows swept the sky;
    Her owlet horns the moon pushed through the leaves

That caught the glare of one great open eye,
   Hesper's, lone gleaming from the western eaves
Of heaven's blue vault.   A chill of dewy air
   Rose from the wave, when Madeline, with change
To sweet composure of her heart's despair,
   Walked slowly from the garden toward the grange.

Now mellow lamp-light filled the spacious hall
   And silence, like the awful hush of death,
Broke only by the night-bird's call,
   Held earth in dusky arms.   The languid breath
Of flowers dropped through the lattice wide and bare ;
   And fancy might have heard the muffled steps
Of long-departed guests upon the stair,
   Like mem'ries threading down the silent years;
And in the heart of Madeline two trains
   Passed ever on, and one was doubts and fears
That beckoned backward to the past with plains
   And many bitter words, at sight of days
That, bearing signs of hope, brought but despair ;
   And one was trust and faith that moved, apace,
From life's spent hopes, upward through paths of prayer.

"A song," her father cried, "a song, my child ;
   To-morrow takes you hence for many days ;
A tender, plaintive song," he said and smiled
   A smile warm with the summer of a parent's praise.

Seated before the ivory bank anon,
   While unseen fingers swept her heart with pain,

She swept the waking octaves with her own,
  And rather wept than sang this simple strain:

1 " Through life's morning fitful, fleeting,
    With its dalliance and caressing
      Waking thought to passion's glow,
  Quick'ning pulse to higher beating,
    All the soul's deep force expressing,
      Breathing on its wish below—
  I am waiting, fondly dreaming,
    On the sands of youth's fair shore;
  Till my boast shall change from seeming,
    Till my stately ship comes o'er.

2 " Now the roseate tints are glowing
    Where the summer skies are bending
      Downward through the depths of light;
  And my once glad dreams are growing,
    Like the day with shadows blending,
      Somber with no sail in sight;
  Still, with dauntless trust I'm waiting
    On the lone enchanted shore,
  Heart and brain to hope pulsating,
    Though no gallant ship comes o'er.

3 " Months and seasons passing, fleeting,
    In their circles waxing, waning,
      Lengthen into weary years;
  Still my heart is wildly beating,
    And my trust is uncomplaining,
      Though oppressed with gath'ring fears.

Hope with ardor warm is burning,
   Beacon midst the silent years,
Still no earnest of returning,
   Still no freighted ship appears!

4 " Many a bark, the mad wave crossing,
   Has escaped and anchored, resting
     'Neath a placid autumn sky;
But amidst the ocean's tossing,
   Where with wind is wind contesting,
     Rides my gallant ship on high,
While with yearnings strange I'm waiting
   On the strand where joys have been,
With earth-pride and wish abating,
   Till my wave-tossed ship comes in!

5 " Evening shades of life are falling,
   O'er the hill-tops darkly brooding,
     Settling slowly o'er the main;
And a mystic voice is calling—
   Sorrow's surcease sure preluding—
     Calling now in hope's refrain;
And my spirit, longing, list'ning,
   Views afar the silent shore
Bathed in morn's eternal glist'ning,
   Where my treasure ship shall moor.

6 " Stars of peace are calmly beaming
   Through the tempest slowly rifting—
     Stars that guide my bark aright,

Lamps of grace whose kindly gleaming,
  O'er the treach'rous billows sifting,
    Drives the dangers from the night.
Voice of power shall calm its heaving,
  Ocean's deep and sullen roar,
And my ship, the waters cleaving,
  Anchor near the golden shore!"

CANTO THIRD.

I.

"THINE own self know," well spake the ancient sage;
  But who can know himself, the heart's wide realm
That stretches, like an untrod land, with rage
  Along its coast of wild dark waves that whelm
In dire dismay who seek their force to stem?
  Where if, by chance of wisdom taught or sent
Of Heaven, one safely hold his storm-tried helm,
  Searching for secret lost to life's intent,
  How must he weep the shame of that dark continent!

Or if, perchance, unsent we pensive ride
  The crested waves far off its mystic strand,
The distant roar of billowy seas and wide,
  Fierce streams, descending mountain paths, command
Our various fears, and awe the desert land;
  And still abide its secrets, tufted plains
Hung round with awful wilds, where thickly stand
  The upas forms, and deadly damp distrains
  The kindly air, till hope expires and fate complains.

Yet hath the strong mysterious God-man's feet
  Compassed in pain that mist world's hidden bounds,
And crimson marked its desert paths, where beat
  The torrid suns of fiery grief, and sounds

Of agony have waked its dread profounds—
  A human soul, path-finding love and hope,
Still pressing on, with loneliness and wounds,
  Amid the night, on furtherest seas to cope
  With death and destined lands to heaven's invasions ope.

II.

Within his study, passion-tossed and racked
With fears that o'er his wine-fired fancy tracked
Their comet paths, paced Rupert Wise and fought,
Through rugged ways and dark defiles of thought,
The fierce-waged battles of despair and doubt,
Till overborne the weary soul wailed out:
"Life is a cheerless passage through the night
And hope a pale, delusive meteor's light
That streaks the gloom with sudden fitful glare,
But dies the moment of its birth.   A snare
Is that desire which kindles passion's flame
To tender thoughts pursue or deeds of nobless claim.
O that I had not known this mocking sin,
Or, better far, that I had never been,
Since life bears not the pleasure of its name,
And since, alas! the future's mystic fame
Is void of softening sheen or image fair
Of other life when doomèd mortals dare!
  The cup that rapture brings to kindred lips
To mine yields bitterness and fierce despair;
  The orb that nightly into ocean dips
Unchains the light anew o'er earth to roll,
  And shakes the tepid dew from morning's urn,

Brings hence to me no morn of sweet control,
  Nor earnest of my sinless years' return ;
The stars that smile to other eyes and shed
Celestial luster on their sight, instead
I see as jeweled daggers in the hands
Of that unpitying, sleepless fate who stands
  Where ends at length the path of mortal fears,
Ready to quench the last of reason's breath
  And shroud in night the fitful, fleeting years
Of suffering man—I hail that sleep of death !

"And yet, God knows, if through yon mocking deep
  There walks a being such as Christians say,
God knows I would have other creed, would weep
  In penitence and, like the humblest, pray ;
But worse than vain were that, I can't believe !
  Ah, there's the rock on which my wish is wrecked ;
Far back as memory's willing pinions cleave,
  Mine was a path by thought of God unflecked ;
And still her woof doth reason blindly weave
  With doubts and strong protests—thus faith is checked

" Yet this, alas ! describes but half my woe—
  To hush my conscience more were base and craven—
I am a slave, a menial cursed and low,
  Of appetite which, like a black-beaked raven,
Feasts night and day upon my vital parts ;
  Nor can I break the Gorgon's hated power,
  'Tis in my veins, I know—the fatal dower
Of our ancestral blood. Toiled by its arts,

My father fell in manhood's gifted prime;
And likewise I must fall; or—deeper hell!—
   Reason must sink, and I shall close my fated time
Not with a dash of wine, but in a madman's cell!

"O Madeline, thy pale and anxious face
   Looks on me through the night—the night that hides
From thee and all the world my one disgrace!
   'Tis false to say my fate with thee abides,
But thine with me; had I responsive will,
   I need but ope the way and thou wouldst come
With all thy wealth of love to keep and fill
   My weary heart.   Stricken I stand and dumb,
Adorèd one, before thy pleading gaze!
   Those tender eyes shall haunt me to my doom,
And thy sweet voice I hear in all my ways.
   O God! this nightshade's death-distilling bloom!
Oft have I cast aside the drunkard's cup
   With awful oath to spurn it all my days;
But ghostly hands have held its madness up,
   While fierce and loud my demon master roared
And showed a ghastly whip of serpent thongs,
Until I yielded what to man belongs
   And on my writhing soul the red wine poured!

" Worse than a thousand deaths of death alone,
   Remorse! consuming hell within the soul;
A tossing waste, a burning desert zone;
   A starless sky where wrathful thunders howl;
A curse of madness on the midnight air—
4

These, more than these, my shrinking sense appall,
And speak anew that awful word—despair!

" Once, goodly legend says, a lonely youth
　Fresh from long wanderings in a desert waste,
Seeking for strength in life—ay, death, forsooth,
　Sat on a tower's black crown that grimly faced
The points of heaven and beetled o'er the massed
　And babbling sons of one wide race, that chased
Through forms and feasts a hope that barely cast
　A shadow on their fading realm.　He sate
Measuring in thought the depth of that black pit
　Beneath the towering wall, and read dark hate
In every face.　' Cast thyself down ; 'tis fit
　That thou shouldst spurn thy soul's untimely fate,'
A spirit spake within ; but idle whit
　Moved not that moveless soul, but dared to wait
Its fated end.　Within me thus there cries
　A voice, loud as the clarion note of war :
' Cast thyself down ; fierce are thine enemies ;
　The pit is fathomless—'tis fitter far.'
But else there cries : ' Not yet, not yet ; suffice
　Their wills ; bide thou death's final battle jar !'

" But must I bear this rankling to the grave,
　This thirst for liquid fires that sate not thirst ?
That youth saw holy grail whose drainings gave,
　Though dashed with bitter woes, a nameless sweet ;
That grail whose draught my burning fancies brave
　Steeps in my heart until it fiercely burst

And heals, yet never heals, itself to meet
   The curse again. I have heard say (O mind,
My better motions, where?) a tree hath leaves
   To heal a wounded heart. Some spirit bind
Them on the bleeding here, and let me sleep
   Sweet sleep, like those Arcadian dreams I find,
When down still memory's vales I lonely go.
   O spirit of the silent hours! O winds,
That deign to kiss my aching, curse-marked brow,
   Where mother's kindly kiss did never fall,
Know ye no kingly spell above, below,
   No healing balm, no gift reserved for all
That stays the flesh and fortifies the mind.
    Say, ebon night, where chance thy steps to fall,
      In all the realm that knows thy darker boast,
Where still primeval shades and silence awe,
    Is there one hiding-place for man defiled?
Deep in Vesuvius' thundering maw
    With stormy waves of ocean o'er it piled,
      Or on the lone and bleak Siberian coast,
O is there peace for me—a fated child?
What sounds? The midnight mocks with scowling brows.
   The wind in idle, bated accents dies
Or laughs a ghostly laughter in the cedar boughs;
   No peace? the tongue that utters that is false; it lies—
Ay, peace there is, of Lethe and of wine!
   Then touch me, Bacchus, with thy wonted spell,
Lay poppies on this throbbing brow of mine,
   This clamorous brood of conscience quell!"

Herewith he filled a beaker to the brim
  With red resolving juice from Bacchus' bower,
And o'er the beaker's chased and crystal rim
  Added the bane of Sinim's deadly flower,
    Quaffed it and sate as in remorseful pain,
  Then rose and lisped, as moved of newborn power :
"Ah, peaceful exit from a dungeon's gloom,
  Now beats my pulse aright, my troubled brain
Its normal force renews, my thoughts resume
  Their wonted trend, and now with might and main
I must work up my treatise on the nerves.
  How fast ambition's scattered seeds do grow !
  To-day they spring, to-morrow leave and blow;
The pupil speaks, and now the master serves;
  With haste my name has gone abroad ; my pen,
  At will, meets those of all the learnèd men.

"Let passion die since timorous faith forbids
And draws its whiter veil, like daisies' lids
At eve's approach; die every wistful thought
Save those ambition's fervid soul hath wrought
To do and dare what meaner minds forego
From sheer consent that reason falls below ;
Dark science hence shall o'er my passions reign
And know my arduous suit, till reason gain
The longed for goal.   Then plucked shall be from out
The garden of my life that tender doubt
That long hath swayed my wish and secret lent
Unto my years its mild atropic scent.
Plucked let it be, though every spray should bleed

And cry, with human anguish, for the meed·
Of longer stay—'twere folly! let it bleed!
Ay, perish leaf and root, and leave but scant
Of memory's self, ambition's goodly plant
Instead grow up a lordly tree, and cast
Defiant front before the driven blast.

"There is no truth in man's evolvèd frame
Of nature or of supernature's claim
I may not know and shall, hence here proclaim
My freedom from all lesser things—ay, more!
Hear it, my ampler powers! there is a store
Of wisdom in the outer world, and hence
No mind has dared to climb. 'Tis high pretense,
But thou shalt tread that dizzy eminence. . . .
Where lore of crucible and astral chart
Has failed of nature's secrets, braver heart
And truer science all shall bring to light.
What rising dreams expand my soul's delight!
That which is named for want of nobler sight
Or fate or death or dire misfortune's might,
Is but of nature's cause and lies within
The mastery of mind, as aye hath been
The ponderous forms of being, soil and tree,
Rivers and rocks and gold and waste of sea;
Be this my task, like those in legends old,
Yet nobler panoplied with strength as bold,
To hunt this dragon of a newer age
Through acme paths and war exterminate wage
On all his hateful brood!

                 "Fade, then, ye dreams
Of soft infolding light; before me streams
The glare of fiercer days, wherein for fame
And sense of proud renown I enter claim.
But stay, my thoughts, why weep this buried love
That will not die?   The singer, fain to prove
In sordid ways and selfish acts, his mind
To mammon wealth and worldly greed inclined,
Hears sighing oft his long neglected harp,
And move him where he may, or join the carp
Of idle tongues, he still must hear its notes
Harmonious, breathed above the miser's dotes—
Reproachful snatches of forgotten lays
That plead return, if haply, to their days.
All broken lies my harp; I hence must hear
But echoes of its plaints, as on the scar
Disrobèd willow-boughs its fragments hang,
As oft before, when pensive love unstrang
Its golden wires.   Farewell, love's riven shell,
Sweet hopes and tender sighs, adieu! farewell!
Another life I enter on ; I can,
I dare the task that crowns and scepters man!"

Loud raps without now reached the student's ear.
  "Who's there, a patient or a visitor?"
"Neither, and yet are both in waiting here."
   With this wide open flew the lattice door,
And one, well known to those who far or near
   Walked through the town, stood in the open way—

An ancient man who bore an antique lyre
   And sang as any chanced to fee his lay.

  " Why up, old man, at this unseemly hour
When spooks and bats for hurt of man conspire?
   You should be quiet in your easy bed,
For withered limbs like yours demand repose."
   "Alas, to find my crust of daily bread
I am content; no home the singer knows,
   And it so falls that, though in street and bower
I've sung the day-dream out, sad and unfed
   I stand before you now.   The generous light
That through your open casement shone
   Bade me come in and freely name my plight.
Pray let me cheer you with a song; alone
You seem; a pittance to the old man thrown
   Will stay his heart and make it glad to-night."

  " Even as you wish, my reverend friend,
   And, to begin with, here's your fee in gold,
   But mind you, in your song no knights of old,
No love-lorn wight, I'm in no mood for these:
Some weird, night-born strain will better please.
   Let it smell of crumbling tombs and church-yard mold,
Or ring with goblin shrieks and wails of sprites,
Or moan with dirge and cant of priestly rites
That mock to shame life's cold and hopeless end."

Then bent that reverend man a courteous knee
   And murmured low: "Your wish I can fulfill;
What these dim eyes have seen, and yet may see

Before they close in peace their heavy lids
To that last sleep, I sing. What is to be
  No mortal knows; occult is that high Will
That ruleth all. The Power that speaks and bids
  The mountains melt, that stills the angry sea,
In His own chosen time will changes bring."

With this the singer swept the wiry maze;
His lips, responding, these weird accents raise:

    1 " Ere the wake of the morn
        Was the pestilence born;
And his foul and dragon-like wings spread afar,
        As he pondered him there
        In the hot fetid air
Over ruin more wasting than famine or war!

    2 " I looked, and a pinion
        Had claimed as dominion
The sea and the isles and the salt-scented gale.
        Quickly turned from the sea,
        Like the wind flieth he,
Till his pall he had cast over earth's favored vale!

    3 " The sun seemed to die
        In his path in the sky,
And wildness and terror filled city and lane;
        The hot tear of sorrow
        Was quenched ere the morrow,
And the dead were interred by the moon's silent wane!

4 "A low, ceaseless wail
        For the smite of the vale
Rose mournfully, ringing from river to sea,
        And the nations in dread
        Watched the plague's wasting tread,
Impotent to stay, but praying the end might be.

5 " Then away slow it crept,
        As the fierce cloud is swept
From the land when war's wild alarums are o'er,
        And a remnant returned
        Where its madness had burned,
But the flower of the valley returned nevermore! "

The song was done ; as though he fain would read
    The singer's thoughts and motives ill ascribe,
The student stood, but quickly thus instead:
    "Ah, thou hast well and duly earned thy bribe !
Go, therefore, now and find what most you need—
    Some wholesome food and wine—then with the tribe
Of Morpheus blest, seek thou the toiler's meed."

The singer hence the student left alone,
    Assayed once more to guide the magic steel,
But languor named the fiery brain its own,
    And bold designs that logic sought to seal
Went fading into dreams and phantasies.
    "Aha!" he cried, " my friends too quickly steal
My sense and touch with velvet sleep my eyes !
    Decreed, I must my task lay by and snatch
From toil an hour of rest, although the prize

Ambition holds demands of all despatch ;
And he who would the wreath of laurels wear
  Must comfort, ease, and slumber sacrifice.
Before the earliest rays of dawn appear,
  With rested limbs and quiet nerves I'll rise
And thus my state will much the theme reveal."

The brazen clock, held firm and safe on high
  By that grave tufted Sire of all the years,
Its gilded hand the lonely hour brought nigh.
  The dial's tale was read: as one who hears
The measured waves of ocean pulsing by
  And sits in dreamy mood, nor recks nor stirs
Till beats the tide his chosen seat around,
  So sat the student, while the waves of time
Echoed along his soul and sleep profound,
  Like rising seas, closed o'er the outer man.
Slow rolled the heavy hours till twice around
  Its measured course the tireless index ran ;
The dying hour unloosed the clanging chime
  And thrilled the sleeper's hot and dreamy brain.

Startled, he woke with sudden, stifled cry
  And bounded from the cushioned seat amain,
Smote through the air, as fiends he would defy ;
  Then sorely mocked his fears with cold upbraid
And murmured : " Sleep is peaceful now no more ; ·
  Such dreams and visions, mingling light and shade,
Yet most, alas! of shade, wove in my brain,
  That shattered loom of thought ! But ere they fade

I must their order seize. Portend they do,
  If ever dreams portend, some evil sore.
Let's see, the land was fair—two woes it knew ;
  Not so—there came a darker scene before !
So—yes ! I have it now, the darkness grew,
  Dim horrors rose and night shut out the view !

"I must at once this vision strange unfold.
  Is it some grim chimera of the night,
Disclosure of that world I am so bold
  As to deny ? or vision meant to fright
And drive me into faith in gods and spooks ?
  If that be so I gladly make the fight ;
Rebellion is my flag. I learn from books
. That dreams are baseless things, the idle fruit
Of chance concern, the freaks of heavy brains.
  I well believe it so, and this 'twould suit
To trace to that old singer's cursèd strains
  Wherein he wailed of death ; but here of late
I am a coward grown and look for evil ;
  If further creed did not eventuate,
I should, from sheer constraint, admit the devil.
  I have a thought, I'll act it out at once ;
There is old De Erl who boasts clairvoyance,
  To test his arts I'll be this night a dunce ;
The feat, I ween, will cost me small annoyance
  And respite give from thought. The place is near ;
'Tis only four, and Stygian darkness reigns.
  I can with ease disguise my face ; I'll wear
This cloak, so none, except at greatest pains,

Could tell whether 'twere man or womankind ;
I'll hawk this reticule as further blind,
So those who see me by the wizard's light,
Will say I seek a patient in the night."

An easy journey through the starlit street
His footsteps brought to where abruptly meet
The stony pave and river's sloping brink.
Here moss-clad oaks and dark magnolias drink
The misty air and drag their pendant boughs
Along the crumbling cliff. E'en when glows
With scorching flame the noonday's sun, a shade,
Like that which filled the Labyrinthic glade,
Mantles the slope down to the river's edge
And flings itself along a terraced ledge,
Midway between the cliff and upper world.
In umbrage hid, like shapeless boulder hurled
From some primeval rift or igneous trap,
A gray *adobe*, cringing, holds this lap
Of flood-disputed earth—a fitting place
To shelter cunning deeds and hide the face
Made gross by sordid thoughts and selfish lore.
Therein from unremembered days before
Dwelt old De Erl, the wizard known of all
Through dark repute, who from his cloister wall
Was seldom seen to stray.
                   Him, burdened sore,
The student unannounced now stood before,
Who rising, surpliced full in textiles rare
And decked with emblem gauds and jewels fair,

In gracious wise, received his youthful guest
And bade him freely name his mild request:
" Great honor 'tis to serve so fair a cause
As that I fondly ween, which hither draws
Your obvious haste.   'Tis granted unto few
Such secrets to divine, but wisdom true
Is justified of all her faithful ones
(The boastful proud are not of wisdom's sons).
A mother fond and doting she, her love
Is kept much as we seek to win and prove
All other preference high ; she must be served
With filial warmth and passion unreserved.
Full threescore years I thus have sought to fill
Her every charge and meet her regal will.
The stars I know and tell their occult law ;
The human senses own my power ; I draw
All secrets forth from envious fate,
And point the soul besieged to better state."

The student heard confounded and amazed,
Such bold unstaid pretense his reason dazed
And stirred the bubbling hotness of his brain,
Till evil visions in perverted train
Floated before his sight and, madness fed,
Into his eyeballs each an arrow sped.
But soon recovering thought and equipoise
He thus rejoined : "Unless too much annoys
The theme, explain, I pray, why thus attired
And at such hour?   Whence have you thus acquired

So rare an art that slumber rules you not,
Nor dreams disturb? Thrice enviable lot!"

"No art is that; I sleep when others wake;
The heavy-hearted most themselves betake
For comfort from my lips 'twixt day and day;
The spirits, too, most aid when night holds sway,
And dearer far to me than sunshine's glow
Are night and yonder darksome river's flow,
When wintry shades, like grim and fabled Thor,
Walk down its liquid path. The ceaseless war
Of midnight torrents dashing past the base
Of that dark cliff, transcends the songs that chase
With ravishment of light and all sweet sounds
The car of day beyond the crimson bounds
Of sunset worlds. But this obtrudes the way;
Unfold your wish, I pray, without delay."

"In me thou seest one whose soul has known
    This night a weary journey through a land
Of changing scenes; a fear now weighs me down,
    I pray you tell me why; open, expand
My sight to see and know the hidden cause.
    If thou be what thou claimest, to command
Were easy task. The wild capricious laws
    Of mind should yield their service unto thee,
    Since of such knowledge thou hast mastery."

"Thou asketh much, yet may'st thy wish obtain
By spirits' help, and these I may retain.

'This table oft has shown enchantment pure;
Herewith 'tis mine departed ghosts to lure,
And call with certain arts the saints from heaven;
These will thy secret thoughts, if they be given,
Link one by one in wisdom's magic chain
Until it pierce the future's wide domain:
Sun cannot shine through wall or pitchy cloud;
No ghost walks from the tomb without its shroud;
Stars, shadows, dreams and of the mind a stint,
Suffice my art—now of your wish the faintest hint."

"Alas, no comfort bideth here! I seek
      What you by cunning would extort: a dream
Disturbed my sleep—'tis gone—to have you speak
      Its essence, show its end and firmly seam
Its parts I came.   But folly's price is paid,
      And as my reason warned, your arts are shams,
Like other juggling priests', and I have laid
      Your ghosts; but know, though twenty drachms
Less one, of mad nepenthe fire my brain,
      I see and kindly take your studied pain."

With this he turned and left the juggler's door,
And soon at home was seated as before,
Seeking to drown his troubled thoughts in work,
But naught he touched but proved a heavy irk.
" No rest, no respite from this dream," he sighed,
" Nor can I tell its order, or decide
Whether to let it do its work and die,
Or seek a further meaning to descry.

Ah! here's a ray of hope: when but a child
 I oft observed the farmer's wife who dressed
Our dairy's store (a gentle soul and mild,
 And full of guileless superstitions pressed),
When troubled what to do or left in doubt
 As to the right of aught in act or creed,
Take up a well-worn Bible, gaze about
 In thought and then at random ope and read;
And if, perchance, the phrase, 'It came to pass,'
 Should meet her eyes, for good or ill decreed,
Forthwith 'twas so, nor dared a soul trespass
 The law.   Here lies that Book; I sometimes read
To prove it false, but if it have one word
To soothe my fear, it shall with joy be heard."

With trembling hands he oped the sacred Book,
And caught the page with quick and searching look;
Amazed he read : "And it shall come to pass "—
O magic sign, flashed through prophetic glass!
When destined years have purged with crucial fire
A nation's life and God has hid his ire,
When lengthening shades portend the peaceful night,
In that mild evening time " it shall be light!"

As sweep the first soft winds of coming spring
Through winter wasted meads, and passing fling
A faint perfume, from Southern bowers stole,
Along the darkling hedge and wooded knoll,
So through the student's inner sense there broke
Sweet memories of his golden days, and spoke

Of perfumed haunts, hard by the paths of love,
Where dulcet voices bade his soul approve
The nobler joys of life.   Though faint they came,
They hushed to calm the siren voice of fame.

'Tis love transmutes the thorny crown to gold;
How brief soe'er its spell or passioned hold,
It fetters ill, bids weak imprisoned hope
Once more attempt its grated doom and cope,
New panoplied, with fate.   Brief, like the cup
Of April clouds, love's chalice holden up
Baptized his spirit's grief, till moved by straint
Of unseen power, he rose and lisping faint
Between his parted lips, he swore an oath,
An awful oath, to ban his curse.   As loath
To let its accents die, lest purpose fail,
He held the words till seemed his breath to wail.

    5

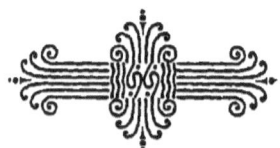

CANTO FOURTH.

I.

THE earliest rays of dawn gleamed on the east,
 And Love's white planet paled and died before
The glow of young Aurora, whose warm breast
  Gave nature joy. Dark ships, with sail and oar
  Of gold, that Argonautic wonders bore
Stood slowly out from day's dim rest
  Into the dusky sky, that isle and shore
Of magic cloudland filled—alas! that best
Of nature's glowing charms should find man still unblest.

Faint from the quay, where man and driven beast
  Groaned through the day, came hum of early toil,
And cry of those whom cruel want oppressed;
  The outcast, filled with shame of night's despoil,
  Shrunk into coverts dark and deeper toil
Of hell's device, to hide the soul beneath
  Its curse, its vileness under that more vile;
Self-stung, like vipers, tasting of a death
That guilty fear saith will not end with mortal breath.

II.

With thoughts alternate, swaying as before,
  Sat Rupert Wise. A rap without now drew
 (66)

Him quickly forth: "Ho there! who storms my door?"
  "A son of Æsculapius, chilled with dew."
He oped, and lo! the form of Jean Pasteur.
  "Good dawning, Doctor! Enter; health to you!'
"And health to you and honors many more;
  A patient well beyond the town has lain
In wavering state. I tarried over night
  To watch his pulse and 'leviate his pain.
In passing near, your very brilliant light
  And, as I thought, a troubled voice within
  Caused me to fear you might be ill. The sin
Of passing by in doubt would heavier fall
  Than that which risks the rousing one from sleep
Even at this hour, for rest the choice of all."

"In truth, I am not well," said Wise, "I keep
  My work in hand, yet find each added call
Must lack because of slowly ebbing strength.
  Of late, I get no rest in sleep; my frame
Thrills like a tensioned lute-string, and at length,
  Unless I get relief or seek repose, must fail—
Vain hope the one; the other voids my aim."

Pasteur in silence heard, but breathed aside:
  "The wine-cup, O that ever saddest tale!
With soul enslaved, what boots the smile of fame?
What's sense of present worth or learning's pride
  Without that nobler hope to light the vale?"

"My dream! my dream!" cried Wise, with nervous start,
  "I had a fearful dream that, palling, fled

Like lowering clouds that angry lightnings part,
  And left my mind with ragged racks of madness
  strewed.   .
To call it back I toiled, but vain my art;
  Now all returns; by chance I catch the thread,
And though to heed such things would ill beseem
  Our better minds, yet, on my troubled head,
  The thing suggests a curious and perplexing dread.
Thus ran my thoughts and thus proceeds the dream:

THE DREAM.

"Alone within a charnel-house I walked,
  Whose ample dome seemed as the heavens outspread;
The constant shades that filled the awful place
  Were somber 'twixt the gloaming and the dread
Of deepest night, so that my eyes might trace
  The aerie outlines of the forms that stalked,
Like sullen sentries, through the silence there.
  My footfalls echoed on the crusted floor,
As when one treads alone deserted streets,
  Or summer waves break on the sandy shore;
Even now my warm blood back retreats
  To think what reeking foulness filled the air;
My heart grew faint and sick, I tottered, reeled
  And straight must needs have fallen, prone and dead;
But one who seemed to mortal men allied
  Sustained with stalwart arm my sinking head
And to my nostrils odorous herbs applied.
  Half borne, half forced by hands the gloom concealed,

I moved along those dim sepulchral halls,
   Then slowly down a wide and gradual stair;
Not long even twilight blessed my aching balls,
   But black Tartarean night and wintry air
Engulfed my frame. Upon my ear there fell
   Beseeching cries that sank to sobbing tones,
Like wintry winds that sigh through ice-mailed pines.
   As down we moved, still deeper swelled those moans
Till all that waste of dark abysmal mines
   Echoed with more than woes of Christian's hell.

" Kissed by that chill, that dread and rayless night,
   My fevered brow grew cool, my strength returned,
And with it came a haunting, voiceless fear.
   I gasped and clutched my speechless guide, who
     spurned
My vise-like grip as manhood spurns a tear;
   My soul was stirred, and in its puny might
Stood forth and through my parchèd lips cried out:
   'Whoe'er thou art, and what, to me means naught,
Yet thou hast led me hither, and I brave
   Thy deepest dungeon and thy darkest thought;
Lead toward thy extreme wish, or fiend or man,
   Though to that blazoned pit thy hidden plan,
Unshrinking hence my willing feet attend,
   That truth to fix earth's sons have vainly sought.

" 'Ah, mortal,' spake my guide, ' thou dost not well
   So much in wrath and madness to declaim,
Thou wanderest not in dungeon or in hell,
   Ay, thou hast sought my mysteries and my name.

My name is called the Past, and yon lone hall
  Which late you trod, the Sepulcher of Time;
Those aerie forms are Centuries, Ages, all,
  Those poisonous damps, that foul and reeking slime,
That life assault and spirit sense appall,
  Rise from the tombs of avarice, hate, and crime,
And crumbling empires in their destined fall
  Heap up their shame and feed the noxious clime;
This yawning gulf, in ebon darkness veiled,
  Unpierced by sight, by mortal unexplored,
Is called on earth *the abyss of human woe.*
  Hither eterne are brought and deeply stored
The griefs of all the years that mortals know,
  Reckoning since man o'er nature's waste prevailed.

" ' These piercing cries, these wild and dirge-like moans,
  Are borne from lands where war's grim form hath rose,
From cities smit with sword and famine cursed;
  Thebes, Troja, Carthage, all have sent their woes;
Yea, Christian years, with history sad reversed,
  From Acre's gates to Khyber's blood-stained snows,
Have made these depths resound with more than mortal
    groans;
  Nor wars alone on heathen heads exhaust,
But in the name of that sweet Christ who died,
  And dying sceptered love, zealots have tossed
To shame and cruel death their kind. To hide
  Their infamy and feed their monstrous lust,
Emperors and kings accusing earth have dyed
  With guiltless blood; hence these ascending groans!

And war's twin sister, direst pestilence,
   Hath fed with agonies of blighted homes
A mad and Styx-like stream, that coursing down
   Its horrid path into this darkness comes.
Thus hast thou seen the sable midnight frown
   That hides the ages dead.   Their fetid tomb
Has sicked thy soul; and rising moans that drown
   All cheerful thought, and name time's certain doom,
Have filled thine ears; from these much may be known,
   And thou may'st read the future's testaments.

" ' In Mizraim's land, the tyrant kings of old,
   Mummied and known through strange-wrought hiero-
      glyphs,
Who that predestined shepherd race compelled
   In bondage sore what years the ecliptic shifts
Full thrice three hundred times its blazing field,
   Builded beneath the desert's sandy rifts
Wide wondering halls, high-domed and ceiled
   With stones granitic from old Nilus's gifts;
Neath pyramidal heaps anon concealed,
   With yearnings raised, and time that lifts
Its light on all, hath scarce their sites revealed;
   Still through their waste the gloom of mystery sifts,
Vague dreams of what is on thy sense annealed.

" ' These be the immemorial woes of man,
   Ever renewed.   But thou, or ere thou rise
To drink again the genial day, shalt scan
   The source of one mad wave that woe supplies

To this black gulf, surpassing all.   Not so
   In long forgotten years; a thermal rill,
Dropping along the pitchy rocks below,
   But swollen now and hot with lava tides
Of mortal and immortal griefs, leaping
   Like those red tongues along Vesuvius' sides;
The Amazon were but a nameless thing
   Beside its liquid leagues.   Deem not unwise
The past since ever thou hast prayed to know
   The secret springs of mortal miseries—
This shalt thou see and trace, companioned so.' .

"Upward we moved counter to those first steps,
   And stood, methinks, upon a massive tower,
But darkness as before.   As when one sweeps
   With straining eyes at midnight's central hour
The wintry sky for one pale star to guide,
   So swept my sight that nether gloom; but vain
The task, save that I saw upon the side,
   That seemed the west thereof, the faintest stain
Of crimson, spreading like the first cold gleam
   Of Borealis on the northern skies,
Or waking in the mind of other dream
   When from the nightmare's horrid chill we rise."

"'That,' spake my guide, 'marks where the living day
   Begins its course; thither our passage bends.'
Swinging a ponderous door, he led the way
   Along an open vale whose slope descends

With gentle sweep toward a stream, whose waves
  Roared like a thousand maddened fiends at war;
The mountains trembled overhead, like knaves
  Before the judgment-seat, their ceaseless jar
Making the dead air quiver like a snarèd bird.

  Onward we moved with slow and steady pace
Through ever lessening night, and still was heard
  The thunderous sound of waves, but less apace
Its volume grew, as lesser grew the tide.

  The quivering air was still, the mountains sank
To gentle hills, and round on every side
  Were pleasant vales, embowered with vines.   I drank
The breath of morning in uncertain light,
  And owned the smell of vintage ripe and sounds
Of revelers and stringed lyres.
                 "To right
My guide turned quickly, and we pressed the bounds
  Of that fierce river, whose unmeasured length,
Our weary feet had tried, and now in twain
  It parted, flowing in unequal strength;
The lesser tide welled from the vintage plain,
  The greater came from marish gloom and fell,
Through pitchy banks beneath the rayless night
  Of hemlock shades; its black and lang'rous swell,
Fat with the reeking lees and oozy death
  That dropped from still-house bins and brewing vaults
Of one black Wizard, seated underneath
  A mountain call the Mount of Rest—but false
The name—drinking from golden chalice human tears,
  And feasting night and day on childhood's flesh,

Compelling those who till the vales, through fears.
 And magic deeds and threat of wizard leash
To waste their wealth for his voracious lust—
I saw, and with my guide the scene discussed.

"As on a cloud my form seemed lifted up
 And borne along the liquid, yielding air,
Keeping the tenor of the valley's slope.
 What sweet forgetfulness of pain and care
Possessed me then! though all in fancy's scope,
And brief; for now the abyss, the vale were gone;
My feet a goodly mountain rested on,
And lo! from out the nether night a dawn
That, breaking, brought celestial splendors forth;
From east to west, from south to north,
The slender shafts of morning sped,
And Phœbus up his azure pathway led
A host of glories, shouting as they went.
Young Spring had spread her emerald tent
O'er all the hills and plains below;
A silvery brightness touched the flow
Of distant streams and threading rills;
While incense, such as sylvan censers fills,
 Perfumed the kiss of every soft-mouthed breeze.
With rapture thrilled, entranced I stood
As westward rolled the rising flood
Of amber sunshine, wave on wave afar,
Where, like the beams of morning's amorous star,
 The dew-drops glistened on the trees.

"Day died, and with a fiery plunge the sun
Dropped through a haze behind the level west,
  Trailing new splendors in his wake;
Day dawned, and as the light looked o'er the crest
  Of eastern hills, I saw the plains awake;
The virgin task of Spring was done
  And motherhood was on the fields that spake
With other voice and clothed in other hue;
  Summer had come, and waving corn
Stood where but late the rank grass grew,
  And through the mild and balmy morn
I saw the glint of spires, the curling blue
    That told where grange and growing village stood;
    Yet still primeval calm was seen to brood
O'er half the world that fruitful summer knew.

"'Twas eve again, and night came on, and day
  Returned when round his path the Titan rode,
And then I heard an unseen Presence say:
  'Look forth again; behold the years have strode
Beyond thy ken!' I looked, and autumn lay
  In wealth of golden glory at my feet;
Paled all the fabled dreams of old Cathay
  Before that world with every good replete.
'I saw rich cities with their clustering fanes
  And stately towers rise through the morning haze,
While far as sight pursued the level plains
  Was still unrolled the pageants' flash and blaze;
Hard by their walls great rivers poured along

Or swept in silent majesty their tide
Through fertile vales where, stirred by labor's song,
  The millions called with easy toil and pride
The harvest forth of fleecy wealth and golden corn.
  Laden with stores and gifts from every clime,
With offerings from the sacred gates of morn,
  From lands that know the happy youth of time
The argosies of trade were on their bosoms borne.

"Anon the sky grew dark, and, pealing far,
  Deep thunders smote the general soul with dread;
I saw the race rise up for glorious war
  And shake the hills with pomp of martial tread,
When notes of trump and drum swelled on the air.
  The lords of spreading fields, palatial seats,
And liveried trains went forth—a knightly band!
  Thrice cruel war when man his kindred meets!
'Twas so—and kindred blood dyed all the land,
  Till in tumultous rout the weaker hurled,
With gory hands, the stronger legions back
  And shook with awful force the listening world;
But breaking thunders in their burning track
  With gathered bolts returned and burst anew
With fury multiplied; the mountains shook,
  The swollen streams ran crimson to the sea,
And all the land put on a drear and ghastly look;
  The fields were waste and bare; while tongues of fire
Licked up the pride that late had made delight.
  Meanwhile a nation's hope must needs expire;

The flickering taper burned with fitful light,
  And then in one great gust of war was lost.
Hark! in that night what heavy chains fall off
  Two races in the conquered land—the slave
And him who held!   Truth unadorned is truth enough!
  I saw the last of that chivàlrous host
Throw down the broken reed of hope and crave
  To die with those more blessed; in mournings deep
They sat amid the ruins of their land;
  But not for long did they in sorrow steep
Their warrior souls, but soon with righteous hand
  Swept down the puny tyrants of the day
And swore for freedom's latest smile to keep
  Their rescued homes—freedom their ancient stay!
And now with peace there came again repose,
  As comes a calm when Boreas' reign is o'er;
Yea, and a beauty in the new land rose
  That shamed the tales of Aiden's fairy lore,
Dimmed all the glory of the old and strove,
  Sun-like, with hatred wheresoe'er it bore,
Till fell on all the radiant light of love.

"Again the Presence cried: 'One woe is past;
  Another darkly falls; part of thy dream
Has been, and part shall shortly be; the last
  Is kindred to the first: divine them as they seem.
Look forth!   I looked, and lo! where virgin peace
  Had widely spread a white and sheltering wing
O'er ripening fields and city's fair increase

There crept, with tigress tread, a treacherous thing
Whose stealthy touch outrivaled war's red hand,
   For, Herod-like, it spared not tender years.
A Memphian wail went ringing through the land,
   A cry that echoed death and all its fears;
The plague, with brazen hand, was everywhere,
   And stalwart men in madness prayed for frost
When summer's heat turned hope to blank despair.
   They prayed, and then, as reckoning folly's cost,
They cursed their God and faithless died, and none
Might pity or remember them; each one
Thought only of himself and of his own.

"And then, methought, ere slumbering dawn awoke,
   The heavens gave frost; the while the shrill north wind
That drave along the level plain and shook
   The pearl-bespangled trees shrieked like a fiend.
The moon, declining toward her quarter next the last,
Sat on a heap of lurid clouds and cast
A pale and death-like gleam o'er all the scene,
   And here and there a star would faintly glow
And then sink back into the night unseen,
   Like eyes that strive to keep the death-sleep off,
Yet less each time of vital essence show;
   Thus in its blessings nature seemed to scoff
At man's deep misery and to mock his woe.

"I sat to watch the multitudes that passed.
Some came with shouts of reverent joy to kiss
   The hem of that white robe and lingering taste,

In open fields and on the mountain-tops, their bliss;
 Others with grateful tears bedewed the way
And blessed the hand that sent the gracious boon
 To re-establish in her rightful sway
Happiness which, like a dove that, soon
 As o'er her home the eagle's shadow glides,
Flies swiftly to her covert and abides
 Till all her trembling fears are past, had flown,
But now returned to bless and keep her own.
 The mighty temples of the land were filled
With thankful worshipers, whose reverent tones
 Mingled in one loud symphony and thrilled
The general heart with praise, and orisons
 Arose from nature's every vocal power.

"I saw a mother, weeping as she came;
 Pale was the sunken cheek where beauty's flower
Had blushed in girlhood's fairer day; her frame
 Was bowed and trembled on her knotty staff,
Like autumn's seared and lately widowed leaf.
 She knelt and kissed the hoar-frost on the ground,
As the poor faithful dog might kiss the hand
 That lays the heavy blow; yet was her wound
Not healed, but rather had its fever fanned
 To wild delirium. Thus aloud she spoke,
Or rather wailed, for pangs of sharp despair
 Slew woman's faith and doubled sorrow's stroke:

"'O faithless one, why hast thou thus delayed?
 Why cam'st thou not in early autumn fair,

Ere death had on my tender beauty preyed
　　And borne my golden treasures hence?   Went first
The orphaned nestlings of my eldest born,
　　The beauteous girl that bore my image erst;
But there was still a prop—a single stay—
　　The younger of my twain, the noble boy
On whom I leaned, who filled my widowed day
　　With peace and all my nights with dreams of joy.
But now his brow is fevered unto death;
　　He knows me not, nor even speaks my name;
His sunken eyes, his hot and bated breath,
　　Burn through my soul with fierce and torturous flame.
And he must die! must die!   My boy! my boy!
　　Why hast thou thus delayed?   This fatal morn
Robs me of my last dream of earthly joy
　　And plants in this old withered heart a thorn
Whose ranklings hand of death alone can end.
　　Come, death; thou art a dear and wished for friend.'

"A low funereal sound rose to my ear,
　　And high along the mountain's sloping side
I saw four sable forms, bearing a bier,
　　White decked as ever lily in its pride,
Toward the wooing silence of a wood;
　　Whereat, descending slowly, far behind
I followed till the moving pageant stood
　　Beneath the boughs, low whispering to the wind,
Of century-gnarlèd oaks festooned with moss,
　　That hung like drooping banners o'er the dead.

Nearer, anon, I drew beneath a cross
   Crumbling with waste of time and overspread
With lichens and the tendriled parasite,
   Where those four sable forms their trust did place
Upon the fresh brown earth, breathing no rite,
   But mute did turn and down the mount retrace
With measured march their steps, leaving to me
   The silence of the place and that white hearse,
Unhonored and unsepulchered.

                        "I see
E'en now that ghostly sight, not ghostly then,
   But soothing like a dream my inmost soul.
Ay, did I dream? The wild flower's modest sheen
   Varied the green of many a mound and knoll
That hid the sacred dust. The trailing vines,
   Jasmine and cypress, round each towering bole
Wrought flowery capitals surpassing those
   Of old that guarded Corinth's proudest shrines;
Moreover, on my sense perfume of rose
   And breath of all rare blooms exotic stole;
While music faint, far off and undefined,
   Yet sweet as voice of love, was on the air;
Two doves, winging that freedom unconfined,
   Staid in their flight and perched above the hearse,
Their plumage shamed beside the whiteness there.
   Ne'er seemed the tomb so calm, so void of fears,
So much to be desired as seemed it then;
   I longed, e'en prayed, to die and lie beside
That spotless guest of death. Madness of men,

  6

Desire for other state, o'erbore the pride
Of school and skeptic faith.

"Long time I stood,
While reasons that my reason knew not of
    Wrought in the dark arena of my mood,
Veering a season toward belief; to scoff
    My doubts forgot; and then a time it seemed
To have my wish of death was granted me;
    But all things ran as ever when I dreamed,
I could not die, yet was I not left free
    To choose my former state of life.

"Fate moved;
I lifted from the face of that still dead
    The white veil's folds.   Well-nigh that rashness proved
My end; the face was fair as ever shed
    Love luster on the world; who had not loved
In life had had no soul for beauty's self!
    A sight was heaven, yet, in a moment, hell
It flung through all the empire of my soul.
    Trembled the solid mount with earthquake swell;
The air grew hot as at the middle pole;
    The pendent moss became all living flame
And every idle leaf became a devil's tongue,
    Hissing with fiendish glee a childish name
Of innocence, unspoken since my life was young.
    I had no power to speak nor strength to fly
More than the chiseled stones that told the dead;
    A thousand years it seemed were passing by,

What time I stood wrapped in that blazon dread,
    But strength returned, and then I fled, but vain
Was flight; those hissing tongues pursued me still,
    Cursing, I know not why, with nameless pain.
Parted the earthquake's mumbling lips; the hill
    Yawned to its everlasting base; I leaped
Into its jaws with smell of fire scath
    On my robes, like they to Zoar fled, when swept
Jehovah Admah's vale with fiery wrath.
    I heard the riven rocks close o'er my head;
Still hurtling down, through voiceless depths I fell,
Happy to hide me in the deepest hell;
    But in that central world's mid-air I woke;
The clammy death-sweat on my forehead stood
And spent my pulse.

                 "What madness have I spoke?
Adjure me that I be but flesh and blood!"

CANTO FIFTH.

I.

SEVEN times, less one, the sun had passed below
  The leaden west, hard on the mystic point
Where cross the circles in the equal flow
  Of day and night. Seven times the sheeny glint
  Of Luna's sickle, mowing without stint
The star-beams, filled the fields of upper blue,
  While some who saw at eve its blood-red tint,
Deemed it the scythe a viewless chariot drew,
Fate driven the while its path of ruin to pursue.

Wild terror swept the city then; the air
  Moonlit, and vap'rous from the river's breath,
Quivered with sighs and accents of despair.
  As though he stood in shape, that monster death,
  And cried each soul forthwith should fall beneath
His dreaded hand, the people trembled all,
  For hour by hour there gained a whispered breath
That for six days within the city's wall
The plague had wrought—how dire the stroke that soon
  must fall!

The populace surged madly to and fro,
  Their pallid faces 'neath the wavering light

Rivaled the white foam on the murky flow
  Of great Missouri, swollen from the height
  Of far Montana's mountains, snow bedight.
Some filled the night with muttered cursings, loud
  Blaspheming that omnific Name whose might
Staid not the plague; and some were speechless cowed,
But the many feared and prayed, putting trust in God.

II.

"What means this madness?" cried a swarthy wight
Fresh from the labors of the forge, "a sight
  To make one think of those wild tumults seen
  When Federal cannon knit their flames between
These hills and yonder stars.   To what intent,
Good friend, is all this hurry, whither bent
  This surging crowd?" he asked, addressing one,
  A toiler like himself, who, still as stone,
With deep reflective purpose stood apart
From that mad human tide.

                              "Why, man, what art
Is this you boast," was held in stern reply;
"Wouldst mock a public fear, or thus decry
  The deep concern men feel for those they love,
  Or are your ears so dull as to approve
No sound like that which fills the air?   'Tis known
The fever cowers in the lower town;
  A hundred cases came to light since eight;
Nor can there be a doubt that all unknown

Amid those slums and haunts of vice the fate
Of quite as many more is sealed."

                     "Alas!
I had not dreamed such evil state obtained;
    'Tis but this moment I essayed to pass
From toil to rest; yet have you well complained
At speech that seemed somewhat to lightness turned.
    How entered in that plague, whose name so late
Was made the butt of learned jest and feigned
    Therein hobgoblin dread? Well done, to wait
The fatal hour before they raise a cry!
    Where are our wise, the keepers of our health,
Who thus have slept with death and furies nigh,
    Feasting their pride and jesting, while by stealth
This hellish minion took and held the gate?
    What does the city do?"

                     " You greatly wrong
Our public men, and more especial those
    Who watch the city's health; for oft and long
They counseled care within. Our outer foes
    They fought at odds that none may fairly rate.
Thus comes this present ill: 'tis shortly learned
    An upward boat put off its sickened mate,
And from that spark the deadly flame has burned.
    What can the city do? Each separate case
Will make its twenty in a fortnight more.
    What shall we do, 'twere better asked, to place

Our lives in safety? what is there in store
    For those mad souls who think to stand and face
The baleful thing? 'tis but to feed the flame;
    The more that fly the fewer fate will slay.
One only course our better thoughts can claim;
    We must be gone, and that without delay.
To-morrow's dawn in this grim seat of death
    Shall find me not.   I wait no prophecy
Of knowing ones; but ere the poisonous breath
    Of night steal, thief-like, through my cottage door
With wife and little ones I shall away."

    "I share your mind, and shall not question more,
Save that I dare to bide the coming day."

Thus passed the eve of that eventful night.
    Meanwhile the town's physicians, watchful, wise,
And quick to hear the call, sprang to the fight
    Like soldiers on the field when foes surprise.
In council brief they tarry while, as wont,
    Their senior speaks: "No matter e'er hath called
Us forth so grave as this we now confront;
    No darker shadow o'er our homes hath palled;
Not when we felt erewhile the iron brunt
    Of savage war seemed hope menaced so much.
    I read our doom as though 'twere writ in lines
Of fire on yonder wall, the fatal touch   .
    Is on the air; but courage that repines
Unworthy is of noble trust. To say
    What shall be done to light the coming curse

Is ours; to meet the plague and, if we may,
　His doings circumscribe and break his brazen force.
My mind is quickly to this point advanced:
　That we at once the people recommend,
At least such as be to it circumstanced,
　That straightly they do fly, and thus defend
The city's present and its future good;
And lest the order be misunderstood,
　And since the case is urgent, brooking not delay,
I would that mounted heralds, swift and fleet,
　Should scour the city ere the break of day,
And cry this pressing word from street to street."

Thus closed the leader, when was heard once more
The mild Acadian voice of Jean Pasteur:
　"To me it seems of wisdom's better part
That we should lend ourselves to duty's deeds
　With partial care, nor all should court the dart,
Whilst few can meet what cause the present pleads.
　As for myself, being exempt from dread
By dint of passing through a former scourge,
　I offer here to lead or to be led
Without delay into the monster's lair
To give him stubborn battle and to purge,
　If Heaven shall please, our city of his doings there."

Like captain, grown impatient with debate,
　While alien feet profane his native land,
The student Wise arose from where he sate
　With peers, and thus prorogued the learned band:

"A prudent course bespeaks itself to all;
　'Tis honor moves to pluck the flower of war,
To walk unflinching to the martyr's fall;
　And yet the future's good requires we bar
Our more insane desires till greater cause
　Shall call us singly to the utmost strife.
In furtherance of a larger end, a pause,
　A husbanding of strength is wise, for life
By life is saved.　Let of our number those
Who know this yellow scourge their skill oppose.
I go, who follows let him follow close."

As when in ocean's dark and middle waste
　There runs along a vessel's crowded ways
The dread alarum cry of fire, till haste
　Makes thought, in that extreme of danger's maze,
Forget its wiser self and madly leap
　For life into the friendless ocean's arms,
So in that hour, with haste and hurrying step,
　Moved by the first dread sound of death alarms,
Thousands poured forth into the fields and wood
　Beyond the fated town, the vaulted sky
Their only roof, their only couch the sod—
　Meaning with earliest light of dawn to fly
For refuge to the mountains' crystal air.
　The evening meal, untasted, kept the board,
Guestless and cheerless, while the feeble glow
Of unsnuffed tapers turned the temple home
　Into the semblance of a tomb now stored

With lifeless clay.   Silence was there, and gloom
  Walked through the unshut doors, sat at the board,.
And spread his dusky couch in every room.
.   .   .   .

Now turn we from the smitten town awhile
  To follow those its children fled in haste,
Happy to find in self-imposèd exile,
  'Mid the wild primeval and the waste
Of mountain wolds, a refuge from the plague.
  The risen sun pours floods of amber light
Along the mist, baptizing cliff and crag
  With filtered beams, and, where the vales invite,
Wasting a lavish warmth ; weird fingers sweep
  The strawy crowns of immemorial pines,
And through the darkling hills the myriad armies weep·
  The everlasting dirge of time.   Long lines
Of weary exiles move to these wild strains
  Along the narrow passes of the hills,
And thankful hearts lift up a psalm that gains
  Upon that deep, sad voice of pines, and fills
The waste, like Israel's song by Egypt's sea,
  Till thousands swell the anthem's loud amen
To lower notes of angel minstrelsy.

As springs the leopard from some flaggy glen
  In Indic jungle to the hunter's path,
So from their coverts armèd peasant bands
  Bound forth and bar the way with signs of wrath,
Their long and murd'rous rifles held in hands
  That knew a cunning half of savagery.

Awhile the startled exiles wondering stood,
  Running their wistful eyes between the sky
And that gray rock and hoary wood
  Whence came a rustic voice with these demands:
"Back, fleeing lepers, reptiles, instantly
  Return, nor dare one further pace to come!
Back with your fevered bodies and your poisoned rags!
  This side that rock you die! Go, make your home
In yonder lordless wild, or back where drags
  Your nursling plague his length through slimy streets!
This, madmen, be our home, this mountain air
  Is pure; these pines distill life's healing sweets,
And taint them you shall not; doubt me and dare,
  Then shall you see how men become a law
Unto themselves, and how defend their own.
  Our weapons you despise? If I should draw
This silver bead against yon hill-top brown,
  Then woe the antlered roebuck browsing there;
The soaring vulture and the screaming kite
  Essay in vain to mock with heavenward flight;
The leaden echoes climb the yielding air,
And bring the treach'rous thief to humblest plight."

A shudder swept the list'ning throng, as when
  On mild October eves at set of sun
A sudden breath of winter touches men
  With icy chill; all felt that wrath to shun,
And fain had turned, but rugged steeps arose
  On either side and hundreds pressed behind.

Some pleaded in the name of right, and chose
   Strong speech, but moved no whit the rustic mind.

A priest, who led the remnant of his flock
   From threatened death, now forward moved and spoke
The leader crouching still upon his rock
   And glaring down with eyes that seemed to smoke
In wrath. Thus railed the priest, with steadfast look:
"Then must we quickly perish! Do your work;
   Our lives are little worth at best. 'Tis well,
Perhaps, they ended thus; we sought to reach
   These heights, as pilgrims seek a shrine. 'Tis well,
Since hope is false, we died! Yet is your heart
   But stone to hold such stern inhuman speech!
Say, in your home dwells there man's better part,
   A wife, and children, meant of God to teach
All nobleness of pity and desire
   For others' good? Then view these helpless ones
That cry for bread. Know you no passion higher
   Than selfish wish, nor honor that atones
For kindness costing aught? The cooling draught,
   Ministered in love, to life's deep river turns
In that fair clime of future good. Fate's shaft
   Is swift; its length the taper quickly burns;
Our whit'ning bones will turn your evil craft
   To bitter use; so shall these infants' cries
Mingle some day with those your own shall make.
   Remember how the Lord in judgment wise
Brought evil for his smitten people's sake
Upon the lands of old, because they said,

'Ye shall not pass.' His hand, may chance, hath led
   Our feet to these your everlasting hills
That you might succor with strong charity,
   And hide our little flocks from preying ills.
Yet make we but the pilgrims' rightful plea,
   A peaceful passage through this public way,
To rest awhile beneath these spreading trees,
   To slake our thirst from yonder spray,
And, if the wish your better motives please,
   We pray the outcasts' mete of staying bread;
If laid upon that rock you hold with care,
   You may depart; to-morrow morn instead
A heap of gold shall greet your eyes, or since
   You fear a poisoned gift, our sacred word
Shall be your bond for such munificence,
   Till hope shall rift the clouds that late have lowered."

Short parley held the leader with his clan,
   And then returned with rifle's front reversed,
Looking more kind and more resembling man;
   Full stern his speech, though calmer than at first:
"Mark well," he cried; "this will we do, nor less
   Nor more: bread shall you find hereon, nor ask
We gold or bond our kindness to redress;
   This fountain and these shades for comfort task
For one short hour, and then with haste pass on;
These hands of ours will see our bidding done."

The peasant left to bring the prayed-for bread,
   The way-worn exiles one by one arrived,

A motley band.   Proud dames and they who led
  The festive throngs of honor, when to give
Delight the queens of fashion strove, must need
  On equal footing with the humblest live
The season of their pilgrimage.   The screed
  Of family, recked of much when fortune smiles,
In shadow of the tomb none boast or read.
The priest beholding one new come with speed,
  Thus greeted him: "I trust, good friend, the whiles
You fly, you hope.   When quitted you the town?"
  "At noon three days ago, and with hot haste
Both night and day have lashed the hackneys on;
  Now will I rest, here pitch my tents and taste
The sweets of sleep; here lay a burden down
  That has since that dread night one week ago
Weighed on me sore.   The babes are ill, and worn
The mother with her vigils and suspense."
  "Alas! it grieves me to advance your woe,
But here we may not dream of rest, but hence
  Must go in one short hour.   Our presence here
Has roused the native clowns to war; our breath
  They seem to fear will spread infection dire;
  That ledge of shaly rock that flanks the brook
Is fortified with rustics armed for death,
  If we essay to pass; but this they took,
That by an hour's space we rest and slake
  Our thirst; while on their guarded rock they lay
A dole of bread, which, they retired, we take
  And then with hurried steps pursue our way."

"Alas! 'tis death before and death behind!
Better to perish in our homes and find
A Christian grave than fall among these wilds
Of want and inhumanity.   Death builds
His wall on every hand; accursed, like Cain,
We rove, and men will aye our suits disdain."

Much pitying him, the holy man replied once more:
  "Be not so much cast down, my son, I pray;
The valleys rich are scarce one day before;
  These reached we shall find plenty, and withal
Full kindly hearts and many an open door;
  There may we safely dwell till heaven let fall
Its boon of frost, and end our evil day.
  But tell me, friend, since you the latest left,
How fared thereto the wretched town? what pace
  Had made the plague—where most his pathway cleft,
Where spared he most, where left his deadliest trace?"

"A faithful tale would beggar human speech;
  The dead are everywhere; from morn to noon,
From noon till eve, from eve till middle night,
  The silent palls go unattended on,
Nor voice of prayer, nor sound of sacred rite;
  Even love, that ever gentle ministrant,
Is robbed of power to keep its holiest trust.
  The stalwart man, the helpless innocent,
Alike are victims made, that lesson teach
  Old as the tomb, scarce hid in parent dust.
The marts are still; the streets, once thronged, are
  hushed,

Save for the tread of flying messengers,
Who, oft o'ertook themselves, fall senseless, flushed
 To sudden death by fever's quenchless fires.
Unwatched, unblessed, the poor and friendless die;
 Their putrid corses lade the deadly air
With newer germs to spread contagion round;
 Beside the son the father falls; from sheer despair
The mother by them both. The priest is found
 Dead by the altar, or the sacred place
Becomes the chamber of his closing hours.
 The kindly simple minister of grace
Within the humblest cot that knows his round
 Is smit, and yields anon his mortal powers.
The fearless son of science, set to heal his kind,
 Unequal to these cruel arts of death,
Not only fails for others' ills a cure to find,
 But falls himself, slain by his patient's poisoned breath.
While thus the stealthy work goes hourly on,
 The swollen river lifts a deep and dirge-like moan."

"Sad tidings hast thou multiplied this day!
 (God stay the plague, else should no flesh remain!)
'Tis well the shadow only haunts our way;
 Christ measures woe in love; the deeper pain
Is hid through shortness of our mortal sight.
 We may not know our loss till milder days
Break on our path and touch of autumn smite,
 Through calms of hope, the dire amaze
That wrecks our sky. Yet runs my thoughts on one
To whom clave hope, so nobly held and done

The task he took, the first to brave the dread;
I mean the stripling Wise, who elders led
To battle with their fate, and fell straightway
Stricken with fever; some believed that day
Would end it. Know you, lies he with the dead?
For much in prayer his name I breathe, between
A doubt and hope—ripe honors may he know!"

"I wist not; yet, when as to leave the town
I made, this tale fell on my ears anon,
Not all unvouched: Three days he lay as dead,
When came a fair, frail girl, who well, 'tis said,
Has loved him from her tender years; and wise,
As well, it seemed, from those first auguries
Of youthful days, so fair his form and face,
So rare his gifts of mind and early grace;
But ere their time for plighting bridal vows,
Through force of false and curious lore that bows
Assent to despot sense and fair device
Of learnèd doubt, he wandered far astray
From truth. Led by his father's evil star,
With boon companions of the bowl he sank
Deep in the shadows of a thralling vice,
Which blighted his and that young life, so near
A part of his. She, faithful still, but frank
With fear, withdrew upon her bridal day
The circlet-scalèd hand; with promise made,
If future days should shed unclouded light
Upon his path, then would she yield him trust
Of wifely love. Late had she sought to write

7

New hope upon her life, and in the shade
Of hills that guard her mother's native vale
Had hid her burning heart.   Therefrom the wail
Of suffering called her to her father's home,
Where, shortly learning of her lover's state,
She came, and by his bedside faithful sate,
And with such care as wife or mother would,
Kept watch; but he, that took nor rest nor food,
Raved in delirium wild, calling one name,
And that her own, as ne'er her love to claim
(So went his rage), or see her face again.
Wildly he talked of how by giant main
They had been torn apart in early years,
And she detained in some far gloom, with tears,
Entreaties, prayers, regarded not, and how
He needs must go to seek her and must show
His love in worthy deeds and abstinence,
And quickly would have risen, going hence,
But that his nurses held him firmly down;
But on the fourth day, being left alone
With only her, he rose and fled away,
So swiftly fled that none might mark or stay
His fleeing form.   They mourn him dead, though none
Dream where or how.

              "That fair young creature soon
Was seized with fever equal his, and lies—
Or when I left lay—in death agonies.
I know no more, save that her name all breathe
In prayer, and hold her love as conquering death;

And when the wrestling few who serve the sick
Would to each other courage speak, or prick
To some unselfish deed or task of martyr mien,
They but pronounce the name of Madeline."

As with a single voice, the multitude
Lifted a lamentation, like the cries
Of those who left Solyma's palaces
To waste in the Judean solitude,
Touched by Jehovah's wrath, while they in tears
And bondage sore fulfilled their captive years:
" How sits she desolate, who once beside
The monarch wave was peerless, like a bride,
Receiving gifts from him whose watery arms
Encircle her, as lover's clasp the charms
Of her new wed.   Heaven's blight is on thee shed,
Thy songs are hushed, thy mirth and joy are fled."

"Ah, *miserere!*" moaned the robeless priest;
"Ah, *miserere!*" sighed each burning breast;
"Ah, *miserere!*" sounded toward the East;
"Ah, *miserere!*" echoed from the West.

CANTO SIXTH.

I.

TOKENS of nature's wrath—fire, hail, and storm,
　　The lightning's brand lit from the pit of hell,
The cyclone's awful breath—swept all the form
　　Of mount and hill, as fierce and loud they fell
From heaven's black-vaulted roof.　Swell after swell
　　The torrents rolled along, and filled the vales
With foam-flecked meres.　Woe! woe! to those who
　　dwell
　　Beside the swift-waved streams!　Woe to the sails
　　On seas high lifted by the equinoctial gales!

The storm was overpassed, and came a calm,
　　An autumn calm, to nature and to man;
Transfusion soft of odorous scents and balm
　　To fit her beauty, faded now and wan,
For silent slumber in the grave by span
　　Of winter's chill and uncongenial days.
A slow and measured throb of music ran
　　Along the pulsing air, as when one plays
　　To sounds of dropping nuts and leaves the iv'ry keys.

Far in the dim and silent autumn woods,
　　Through paths with spiteful brambles overgrown,
And deep and long untrodden wilds, where broods

The night-hawk's mate and plaintive wail and moan
Of whippoorwill and owl disturb the noon—
  So deep the gloom beneath those tangled boughs—
Wandered, with starless wish and mind o'erthrown,
  The student Wise, his darkly knitted brows
  And trembling frame bespeaking pain and broken
    vows.

II.

"Dreams, dreams, a mocking frenzy murders thought,
  And reason's throne supplants with pallid fear;
The downy plumes of light impending air
  With mountain heaviness compel me here;
A giant's brazen arm were futile fare
  Against these links a thralling fate hath wrought.
Bides there indeed a twofold essence here?
  Or am I but a part of all I see—
Insensate brother of the rock, a sphere
  Of action filling higher, yet less free,
Than yonder clambering vine? To caprice wrought,
  To end of folly and the base desire
Of some dread spirit reigning in this wild?
  And art thou, Solitude, perfidious sire
Of all my woes, and hast thou hence beguiled
  My wandering steps, veiling an evil plot,
To bind me to the rock of cold disdain?
  Fulfill that wish; thou canst not nobler crown
Nor ampler wealth confer. The Titan's chain
  My heritage, I ask no more renown,
Nor sighs my soul for pleasures sweeter got.

"Somewhat there is, in truth, that men call life,
     A spirit essence, flung from unknown heights
Through depths and darkness into fateful strife
     And conflict with unequal force, that smites
With fierce, disloyal hand its own defense;
     That stays to shame prepense its own delights,
And buys despair with mind's immortal recompense.

"Is this with me that being's primal morn,
     Cast from the womb of silence at her will,
Or have I palsied lain while tireless years
     Have run their course, yet, nathless, suffering still?
There seems a past, a past of doubts and fears,
     But of its changes, seasons, naught is borne,
Save that I lived and something lived beside,
     Or else I saw myself move through the light
And knew communion, while a less'ning tide
     Of passions, bosom born, returned delight,
     As on yon lakelet's face the mountain glories burn."

Thus moved the student's wavering mind, the while
He sat exhausted on a mossy pile
Beside a sylvan lake fed by two brooks
That wore their channels into eddied nooks;
One sent from distant fenland's grassy pride,
The other murmurous from the mountain's side;
Which, when the errant breezes ceased their call,
     Intoned the harmony of falling leaves.
These heard he: as familiar voices fall
     Upon the ear and reach the heart that grieves

Its memories dead, so fell the liquid sound
And quickened feelings that for years had swound.
As in its purple morn the soul rose up,
And drank again from childhood's dregless cup,
Dreamed over dreams that blessed the sinless boy,
And cried aloud the frenzy of its joy:
    "Hail, woodland melodies, preludes of hope,
How swells my heart once more to hold in view
    That goodly sight, the mansion of my sire;
The whitening fields, the meadow's crown of dew,
    The haunted hills, aglow with sunset's fire—
      Alack, the shame! my life's unfruitful scope;
Alack, the evil fruits that folly bore!
    But I must suffer, since 'tis so decreed,
And since 'tis being's nobler ends that wait
    The issue of my suffering state, and plead
Supernal wish and conquering trust create,
    I lowly bow, the scepter kiss, the King adore.'

A shadow, other than the mountain's, fell
Athwart the surface of the lake; the dell
Re-echoed other than the streamlet's voice,
And in that far secluded spot the noise
Of human footsteps caught the student's ear.
When furtively he glanced and saw him near
A hermit strangely clad, with shaven head,
Who at the sight of Wise had quickly fled,
    But that he rose, signaled desire, and cried:
    "Stay, brother—if that word conveys the thought
That forms my wish—kindred, or being's shade,

Return, abide, and be companion of my care;
Here is my. rest; my vows henceforth are paid
  Beside this gray and ancient rock.   Come, share
    My thoughts, and cast with me thy lonely lot."

Hereat the hermit staid, and thus replied:
  " Mortal thou art and kindred to my sense;
'Tis twenty years since mortal face I dared,
  Yet will I turn ; thy frail, emaciate form,
Thy sunken eyes, thy voice by fast impaired,
  Forbid my fears and hate of man disarm.
    Speak, if I may some boon of good dispense."

Wise. " 'Tis not the body, but the mind that cries
  For food, for surcease from its heavy weight.
Sit thou beside me here, and enterprise
  An arduous task."

Hermit.   " But first, I pray, relate
  Why driven so far from human haunts? why
In communion as with morbid thoughts and fears?
  Surely it is not oft thy wont to fly
So far; nor seems it me thy mind appears
  In wonted force, for thine is fair estate."

Wise. " Truly I must be more than what I seem,
  But thought has lost the golden key that turned
The bars of fate,that faint soever gleam
  Of peace might visit one self-loathed and spurned ;
But what I feel or know—perchance, I dream—
  What matter? felt or dreamed, 'tis easy learned."

Hermit. "Mine ears are thine; so long since human voice
Their sense approved, and now with hearty choice

Wise. "Ah, there bethink me! patience, rest awhile!
Whence are we, hermit? more than wont of man
Thou seemest wise. Whence? whither? whose at last?
When, like the summer winds or gust
Of winter, sinks our sensuous breath,
Hushed in the deep and mystic silences
Of those far voids from whence alike they rose;
The winds sleep in their sea-girt caves again,
Dirgeless and unlamented by the waves
Whose tawny, sun-tried cheeks they wantoned o'er,
Until they crimsoned softly here and there
With sunset hues, or blanched beneath the glow
Of silver stars. But is there naught that lives
Remembered of the winds' wide errant course?
Of sylvan wilds or trellised garden bowers?
Of rattling fleets of reefed merchant sails?
Of dalliance at soft eve or luteful sounds
At early morn? of lovers in their trysting-place;
Or merry childhood on the village green;
Or manhood everywhere, in peace, in war?"

Hermit. "Nay, life is not in memory with the winds,
Nor echoes through their slumb'rous cavern homes;
Subtler its essence than the ether wave,
Fleeter than fancy, rises to a higher rest,
To sleep, to wait, to wander forth no more,
Until the end, removed from earthly wisdom

In the boundless reaches of the soul's hereafter,
When, all things restored—like to its like,
And god-like to itself—eternity its firm
And changeless order shall begin."

Wise. " Where are those dim ethereal spaces,
Where the fitful breath and fiery thought of man
Repose, abiding that eventful hour?   Science
Cannot discern their pillared fastnesses
Nor tell their vaulted dome, nor yet
Hath hinted that they be.   Winging a swifter flight
Than condor of the Andes through his realm
Above the waste of Chimborazian snows,
Thought goes upward through the blinding maze
Of planets, suns, and *nebulæ*, whose fiery haze
Unrolled, in fragments, from the everlasting scroll
Held in the great right hand of God,
When chaos kept the formless deeps below.
Orb after orb pales in its lengthening track,
While others dimly blaze and wheel before,
And some, girt round with many moons,
And others—flaming suns themselves—compelling
And, in their turn, compelled by other suns
As satellites, and each a different sheen,
Swift on ecliptic marches, centric and concentric,
Making a conturied day of rainbow light.
But, staying not, the vision plunges headlong
Into sunless, starless wastes, black with the pall
Of night, primeval night, only to gain,
When myriad million leagues are measured through,

A sight of white-flecked skies in deeper wilds—
Monotony of wide creation's awful self!
Where, then, bold wanderer of the night
And pathless fields of star-flecked gloom,
Where is thy lost brotherhood, where the place,
The far Valhalla, of their long retreat?
And where the hostage of the dust
That once compelled their stay with sweet restraints?"

Hermit. "That which thou seest is but the tessled pave
And archèd door-way of our Father's house;
Hath not the Power that binds each planet
To its sun, and these to nature's ancient heart,
Hath not he scope to build him otherwhere
And otherwise, beyond our sight, a spacious rest?"

Wise. "A handful of ground and molten sand,
Shaped into kinship with the visual sense,
Stole wondrous secrets from the voiceless night,
Turned doubt to faith and faith to doubt,
And made our lives seem less and nature more;
And what erewhile appeared a creamy stretch
Of white coast lines, along which spent
The furtherest waves of nature's starry sea,
Before it broke and fled, and in its place
Rolled still a fiery tide of orbèd light;
But spectra of those furthest discs
Tell but of kindred elements, nor hint
Save of such forms as mundane wisdom knows:
The crystal dust we grind beneath our feet

Is like in kind the hissing lava streams
That course the hearts of mightiest suns;
And not the tiniest sphere of evening dew,
Or minim of the ether sea, but sisters
Those vast firmaments, attenuate, void,
Infolding solar fires.   What then?
Shall spirit quit the ponderous forms
And gross restraints of matter here,
But to resume them otherwhere? or cast
One mold, and take its flight but to be clogged,
Though nobler wise, with cumbrous life again?"

Hermit. "Matter is but mind's accident; the dust
Hath been full many thousand times alive
With different sense and pulse.   They who,
Following the divine decree, lord o'er the earth,
If phalanxed like an army on its march,
Would reach well-nigh the ecliptic's blazing belt;
While those who have gone forth since time began,
If marshaled thus, would overlap Arcturus
And the stretch of wild Centauri's realm.
The foremost moving thus, perchance, might sight
The gates of that fair city in the wide beyond.
If each had borne his death-devoted clay,
Then had there been a waste and wreck of earth.
Knowest thou matter? hath yet a human eye,
With aid of burnished glass, beheld an atom?
In clusters seen, yet not in essence known;
Spirit thou seest not nor matter yet:
There resteth mystery for the wise."

Wise. "Hermit, thou talkest as a god might talk;
Thy words are wise and fair; I could well think
We walked in old Palermo by the sea,
Or sat by Athen's walls in those old days
When spake Aristo's son his deathless words.
Go on; though weak, I hear with joy."

Hermit. "Nay, lade thy mind not now with such high
    theme,
    Nor bid me, man unlearned and recluse, prate
Of things removed from human sight and dream:
    Turn for a time to thoughts of humbler state;
A season, when thy wonted strength returns,
    We will such lofty things attempt.   Now waits
Within my cot a frugal meal, and burns
    A fagot fire upon the humble hearth;
A couch is there of silken grass, and spread
    With fabric of the mountain cougar's swarth.
There thou shalt rest thy frame and, breaking bread,
    Remain till strengthened limbs may bear thee hence;
Or, seeming good, a longer season stay,
    And taste the freedom of the wild and fence
The heart from earthly care, or make it aye;
    And he who faileth first shall be to him
Who thrives a care to lay him in the dust
    And shed a tear, chanting a lowly hymn
Above his grave.

                    "Thy grief and ail, I trow,
Are of the heart: ah! there are songs within

The compass of these wilds and winds that blow,
Bringing a solace to the heart that sin—
 The raven torturer, sin—has sorely torn.
Amid these sylvan shades, as in the vale
 'Twixt Tigris and the Gihon's wave, at morn,
At eve, God walks; and when the leaves do fail,
 As now, and gorgeous carpets clothe the hill
And woven arras of the sunlight drops
 Around the woods, then choiring spirits fill
The leafless groves and, in the hallowed stops
 Of organ winds, glide softly through the light."

With troubled, yearning heart and upward gaze,
 Like sailor's through the misty morn or night,
Searching for beacon o'er the harbor place,
 The student through his darkly clouded mind
Strove for the light of that fair-limnèd peace;
 But ever backward turned, made thrice more blind
 By what he felt; till that faint memories
Of what his unshod feet had hither moved,
 Broke on his brain, when with weak voice he cried:

"O dweller in the waste, wise art thou proved
 And happy in thy lot! Since thou didst hide
First in this lonely wild, say hast thou seen
 A maiden bound or wailing 'neath the pines,
With tresses like the chestnut dawn and sheen
 Of lily crocus on her cheek? O shines
The sun and comes again the dewy eve,
 And I no trace of my dear love descry!

May be, I vainly hope or, wandering, leave
   The truer path; then tell me, has thine eye,
In lowly vale where bending willows weave
   A woof of green before the quiv'ring sky,
Beheld a bleeding heart, pierced with a thorn,
   And ruddier than its kind? That is my love's;
There she has died, and Dryad sprites have borne
   Her to their sisterhood, 'mid beechen groves
And aspens whispering low; and near it saw'st
   Thou but a broken stone, like chrysolite
Wrenched from the parent mass by glacier's frost
   And worn beneath its icy heel? O sight
For mortal eye! that stone is my hard heart,
   Its blessing that it lies beside her own.
When shall this life's dark prison walls dispart
   And let me forth—to death, to life? Atone?
For what? by what? for this foul deed of mine,
   Whereby I slew two hearts? Methinks I hear,
As from a far-off day and from a shrine
   Hard by a murm'rous fount, one sound that mocked
And mocks me still: 'Atone! the blood! the blood!'
   Ah me! it seems the sable nurse that rocked
My dameless infant years chanted the same
   So long ago!
                "O, hermit, is it true?
Is this that mount? Ay, babbler, tell thy name,
   And let the curse descend. Too late for you!"

The hermit answered not, seeing his thought
   Wandered in mental night, and that he seemed

Distressed with hunger and a thirst that wrought,
    Its desert dryness on his bloodless lips,
Parching the feeble words, and so he deemed
    It better to repair at once with this,
His charge, into the cot, that distant seemed
    Hung like an eagle's aerie in the slips
Of weathered rocks—the mountain's wasting heart.

So he the student lift, nor moved amiss
    A muscle in the act, and with the art
And strength of mountaineer bore him aloft,
    And laid him on his couch, and, brewing tea
And toasting barley bread, grown in the croft
    About the cot, he had the joy to see
His guest partake, look up, and calmly smile;
    Then, settling on the mossy couch, fall soon
Into a slumber gentle, soft. Meanwhile,
    The hermit watched and wondered of this boon,
Not all delight, yet not displeasing quite,
    Which fortune charged him with. The sense
Of loneliness so long had made its night
    Within that this became his recompense,
That all the world of waste and rock, of wood
And stream and cloud, yielded him brotherhood.

And who was he, that hermit of the waste
    Who twenty years had shunned the face of man,
And talked with winds and clouds, and lightly chased
    The elfin sprites of fancy through the wan
Of autumn twilight, and had built a shrine
    Beneath the nightly stars to worship God?

Who heard him walking, in the eve, and shine
    Of morning suns, through goodly vales; who trod
Himself the ways of prophet, sage and great,
    Of ancient days, abiding thus in nature's sight?
What blight destroyed his early flower? what fate
    Impelled him hence, a loveless, friendless wight?

A melancholy, like the mist that time
    Spreads o'er a marish glen and lifteth not,
The child of some swift youthful crime,
    Through sore remorse, had made him choose this lot;
That crime, his name and all that told
    His past—a mystery, like himself. He spent
In simple toils and musings manifold
    On nature's goodly frame the days' content—
At first through fear of man, at last through choice,
    And so he dwelt, and older grew and wise
In nature's lore and thoughts of God, whose voice
    He heard in three great books—nature, himself,
And that which came by fire. Then what surprise
    That, dwelling thus so near the heart, the self,
Of nature, he should catch her words, and turn
    Them into grateful songs? for oft beneath
The star-bedizened vault he walked, with yearn
    Of holy passion in his soul and wreath
    Of starlight round his head, chanting low,
Sweet anthems—epics of the wood and strains
    According with the harping pines below.

Thus, when the student slept, and with her trains
    Still night was passing through the cloudless sky,

Touched with a kindred sorrow for the youth,
  He wandered forth, deeming the Healer nigh,
And to the mountain pine murmured his ruth:

      1 O dark-browed pine!
So like the shade of a grim old god
Uprising against the starlit blue,
      And art thou a god,
      And I but a clod?
Thou weepest much, and I weep too,
      O dark-browed pine!

      2 O dark-browed pine!
I must weep tears, and tears that are hot—
Hot from a heart that ever hath fears.
      Ah, my tears are hot!
      But tears thou hast not;
Aye, weeping, thou never hadst tears,
      O dark-browed pine!

      3 O dark-browed pine!
Thou hast a faith—a faith of thine own—
Or else thou hadst quit the mountain rock,
      In storms that have blown
      With a wild winter moan,
Else hadst thou reeled with the thunder s shock,
      O dark-browed pine!

      4 O dark-browed pine!
And thou hast a hope; thy somber shade
The lightning shall kiss with lover's thrill,

Nor ever that shade
Know the woodman's blade;
Thine are the years of a century still,
O dark-browed pine!

5 O dark-browed pine!
I hear thee oft in the deeper night,
Sobbing aloud in a dismal strain,
As never I might
In that deeper night,
Sobbing with all but a human pain,
O dark-browed pine!

6 O dark-browed pine!
Is it all because thou hast no tears
That thou wail'st so with an endless plaint?
Then half of thy years
For the gift of tears,
Though thy years were the years of a saint,
O dark-browed pine!

7 O dark-browed pine!
This night, as never thou weptest yet,
A wandering soul in the valley dim,
Though his sun be set,
And the night-dews wet
The fleeing sprite—weep aloud for him,
O dark-browed pine!

CANTO SEVENTH.

I.

NOW on the mountain stood the white-robed Morn,
And waved a beamy scepter, while was borne
Far through the waking vales heraldic notes,
And signs of her approaching car. As floats
The eagle upward, slowly round and round,
The mist went upward toward the blue profound
Of star-deserted heaven. The pale, sweet moon,
Like hunter's horn at height of sultry noon
Suspended by the stream, hung in the blue
Below the birch-trees' arching boughs that grew
Along the mountain's western slope; a calm,
A deep, soul-soothing hush, as when a psalm,
By early worshipers devoutly sung,
Dies from a great cathedral and among
Its many pillared aisles broods voiceless prayer,
Hushed all the mount and all the upper air.

II.

While thus the virgin day began her course
Through cloudless sky and nature's calm, perforce
Of nature's sweet restoring law, awoke
The student to the light that once more broke

Upon his soul's unclouded sky.   The shade
Was gone; the fever's trace, the bane that made
Of thought an aspic's bite, were gone, and lo!
The soul beheld itself and knew its woe
Unshadowed by a dream; and quickly read
A hasting doom, and heard not far the tread
Of baffled death, stealing, like tigress on the prey
Chance struck by hunter's dart and fallen in the way.
Moveless he lay, while trembling sunbeams kissed
His bloodless lips, sweet emblems they of love,
Eternal, mystic light, that leaping from above
Struggled to force his soul with mercy's ray
And kiss its darkest stains of guilt away.

Seated beside the youth, the hermit saw
His mind reclaim its throne, and felt the awe
Of fast approaching death.   In kindly tone
He asked that dying wish be said or shown,
When in a clear though slowly failing voice
The answer came: "Hermit, I much rejoice
That thus my end draws nigh; kind fate reserves,
I trow, some good that lucid hour is mine
In which to die; and yet how much deserves
My soul a darker end; but heaven or fate
Or else, however named, is kind.   I wait
To know the utmost of the truth divine
Or darkness of the night that mortals dread.
But hear my tale, and then, if thou hast read

In nature's goodly lore or elsewhere found
A solace or a cure, ere that dim bound
Of death I pass, speak to my soul a hope.

"What Summer's frugal care nad gathered up
Autumn with lavish hand was strawing wide,
And gloried in the waste, till wasteful pride
Had wrecked and left her sad—November drear,
The mystic twilight of the fading year;
The season night—so says the chronicleer—
An infant's wail broke on the stilly hour;
A life—my life—with its dark-fated dower,
Woke to the light, while hers who gave me birth
Went outward toward its rest—equal its worth
I fondly trow, yet lost that hope hath been,
Left aye to die in starless night of sin;
Brief on me beamed a father's face within
A spacious house, ancestral home of wealth,
With lordly grounds, oak-girt, where love and health
Might wedded dwell, and bring forth fresh delight
With every changing hour.   Fair to the sight
The grassy lawns and breezy groves alive
With warbling birds and bees that to their hive
Bore honied treasures all the day.   Shame fills
    Mine eyes with tears! for then my soul was free;
No cygnet's down was whiter.   From the hills
    That rose, like islands, in the ether sea,
Minerva-like, a streamlet burst; pure white
Its waters, sparkling in the liquid light,

Yet not more pure than those white thoughts that erst
Upon my spirit's forming vision burst.
I heard the thunders walking through the hills;
   I saw the panting clouds chased by the wind,
And saw the lightning's burning blade that stills
   The heart, even as the hunter's bleeds the hind,
Slash through its shaggy sides, until it bled
A torrent like the sea; and then that thread
Of limpid water grew into a tide
   Of turbid blackness, groaning as it passed.
The judgment's thunders—shapes of wrath—with stride
   To shake the mountain-pillared world, have traced
My soul; the fiery brand hath parted quick
Joint, marrow, and the secret life, and thick
Hath rained a scorching dew—pollution's shower
That choked the limpid wish to this my fatal hour.

"But backward let me turn—a summer day,
A rare June day, or had been such, dare say,
   Death walked within the lordly house; my sire
Obeyed, and hence strong men bore to the grave
   All kindred clay of mine, save one not nigher
Than fourth in blood. A thoughtless whisper gave
   My ears that day a truth not understood,
   Alas! too deeply since, for through his blood
Ancestral came my father's fate—a curse
Of appetite, that fed, grew ever worse
From sire to son and bore him to his doom
In middle life. Short while within my home,
Now doubly waste and haunted with the gloom

Of long distressed, I tarried, choosing me
(Such course the law permitting by decree)
To dwell my youth with him my nearest kin,
And so I journeyed toward the west, and in
A home no whit less proud in boast or name
Than that I knew before began to claim
An equal hope of life.   My early woe
Was soon dispelled, for in the ample show
Of love my childless kinsman made I grew
To feel a higher joy than e'er I knew
In years before, and else a well-spring burst
Within my life; a fount of peace that thirst
Of unfed wish assuaged, for hard against
My kinsman's lordly lands another fenced
With equal pride and equal cheer dispensed.

" So fell a time in those first days, when through
Adventurous thought, chasing delight where grew
The hedge-rose and the brown thrush made its nest,
I chanced to hear, in childhood's fairy jest,
A little rippling laughter and a song
    That gurgled softly, leaping as from tongue
Of bird or elfin creature of the field.
I stood in transports, till my sight revealed
    The sweetest wonder of my dreams: a maid,
A tiny, elfin creature of the field,
    Our neighbor's eight-year-old, had strayed
Into the sunlight and the open waste
And, like the summer warbler, with a taste

As dainty as herself, was mocking there
The songs and laughter of the birds.   O air
Of summers gone! O dreams of perished bliss!
O hopes deferred! O love's first balmy kiss!
    Return, return again!

          " Life grew apàce,
And hope went upward, like the lark, to face
The mighty sun and revel in his fires.
What happy days went by! and with desires
And benedictions deep as life could hold
Grew that sweet maid, and she was mine.   The fold
Of month on month and year on year, until
Our lives did one fair book of pleasure fill,
Made only more our souls each other seek,
And mine was lost in hers and felt to speak
Her purer thoughts; yet, as the tendriled vine
Leans on the oak, hers seemed to lean on mine.
As some lost deer in lonely forest wild
Drinks from the placid brook, and stands beguiled
  With semblance of himself upon the wave,
So drank I from the light of her deep eyes
  And saw such stainless vision as they gave,
And knew my nobler self in semblance rise
  And float their placid fullness through.

            " To dwell
In that aureate glow, with her my sun,
  My virgin hope, far from the raging hell
That woke my curse and fired my blood too soon

And scourged me down my fated path, had wrought
My crown and made my bliss; but kindly thought
My kinsman moved to plan a fair career,
An end whereby a goodly fame should rear
My fortunes high; and so I made to seek
In learning's halls of wisdom's gifts a share,
And hence should go at lapse of one short week.

" 'Twas on an eve in that soft season when
The bearded barley, ripening, bows its head
To sweep of sportive winds; the broad sun then,
Creeping along the silence crimson red,
Had dipped its edge behind the emerald sea
Of forest glades beyond the river's bed,
I walked with Madeline along the lee
Of that brown waste of waving corn, and free
And light our hearts as softest zephyrs' breath
That stirs the fringèd myrtle in the groves
Faun held and sacred to the restful gods.
The roving quails puttered in every heath
And bluebirds in the locusts told their loves
Or danced along the daisy-tufted clods.
Above us bent the patient, dewy heaven,
Like tender mother in her pride; two stars
Anon, like mother eyes, looked on us twain;
Her hand was in my own, and we had striven
To pierce the deep, sweet mystery that bars
The future from the now; with yearn and strain
Of hope her lustrous eyes had sought the way
Adown which walked the ghost of fading day.

"Vermilion splendors burst a moment forth
    And half the evening's vastness penciled o'er,
        Hiding the light of those twin stars in fires
Of mightier glow.   Omen of goodly worth
        We read in such response to love's desires;
    And holy thoughts leaped to my lips and bore
Their transports through my soul, till speech was dumb.
    Save in one mighty word, breathed till the air
        Was tremulous with passion's sacred sound.
A quick, sharp cry from Madeline made numb
    My senses for a time; I could but stare,
        Seeing her fly like doe before the hound,
        Till, casting sight along the shadowy ground,
I saw a serpent of prodigious size
With maddened hiss and fiery, darting eyes
Glide from the rye and pass between us twain.
With fearful thought and pang of inner pain,
I forward sprang and caught her to my breast
And stilled her fluttering heart with lover's zest;
Yet liked I not the shade that held her brow,
As some fore-fruit of ill, nor forth did go
With morrow's dawn, when that for four long years
I took my leave.

                "That morning marks the line
'Between what I had been and what I am.
Ah, could the sailor know the maelstrom stirs
    The sea within his path, he durst not quit
The land-locked harbor for the wave; so mine
        Had proved a happier fate, a nobler fame,

To walk in that idyllic dream and sit
   In that manorial shade, knowing no blame.

"An ancient classic seat beyond the sea
   Received me to its grim and ample walls,
Where busted pride and living fame purvey
   All noble thought, till wisdom's portion palls
Through goodly store and school-man's lavish care;
   Yet aught, though all I failed to heed the cause,
Weighed on me that the form bore not its share
   Of vital truth.   Tomes, cycles, barren laws
   And endless reckonings, doubts, perchances, flaws
And stresses of the mind, filled not the soul
   That early read the volumes of the field
And measured by the sunshine and the roll
   Of boundless floods the problems of the world;
   That knew but love as tutor, nor to yield
Had ever thought a tittle of its dream.
   Into a semi-Arctic silence hurled,
As from a luteful land of tropic gleam,
   I seemed to yield, and wrought in mines
For gold and gems and deemed me wise to hold
The tender sense in awe of that more bold,
   Which delved unfed, save on the husks and rinds
That strewed the desert paths of Christless lore.
But pleasure oped her gates and spread her store
   E'en in the desert world, and youth to youth,
In friendship bound, held up the fatal pledge;
   Convivial laughter and the bowl put truth,
If truth, indeed, engaged, aside till edge

Was off the finer sense, and blunt and dull
The nobler wish.   Restraint was not, nor voice,
  Nor Orphic string the frenzied thirst to lull
And drown the sirens' song—there was but choice
  To leap and die, seeing no Ithic purpose bound.

"I felt a demon rousing in my blood;
  A fiery hell was kindled in my brain,
And loud from out the silence woke a sound,
  A sound of doom, but all too late; the chain,
The heavy gyves were forged and sealed; I stood
  A slave, as all my sires had been, and vain
The voice; for pleasure laid her balmy hand
Upon my.brow and far my native land,
  And all dear things it held, drifted from sight.
At length I woke in helpless pain and knew,
  O God! I knew my dungeon and the blight
Of manhood's hopes, and love and mem'ry threw
  Their torturing sweetness o'er the troubled brain;
The serpent hissing from the rye, the face
  I left with sadness wreathed, slew me with pain
Of mad despair.

                    "I rose at midnight's hour,
  With oath to live, and fled with frantic pace
Through olden lands and cities boasting dower
  Of unrecorded pride; beside all seas,
Through holy haunts and temples of the gods
  Whose very names are lost, with listless gaze
And longing after what I could not say,

I wandered by the space that Phœbus plods
Three times around his orb-encircled way.

" Rome's red palaces, Arcadia's misty hills,
   Old Gaza in the desert's heart, the waves
That lap the Ormuz coast, where morning fills
   Her wasted urn, have heard my sighs, and graves
Of swarthy kings in Ind and Aiden's groves
   Have wooed me for a time to think of Brahm
And happy rest, where Soma's river proves ·
   The solace of all mortal ills.   The calm
Of Ida's wood, the mount of Thessaly,
   Beguiled me from my bondage for a time;
Ay, I have laid me down where old rhymes say
   The Titan, doomed to expiate his crime,
Three thousand years in chains and torture lay.
   Caucasus, on thy rocky sides I sate
And watched the green light of the meteors play
   Upon the streams that feed the Euxine's wave;
To Joppa turned and through the valley gate,
   Esdraelon, passed where Kidron's waters lave
The mount of sacred name; the wailing-place
   Of Judah by the ruined walls I pressed,
And from Golgotha's dark retreat did trace
   The wrinkled hills to Olivet—but rest,
The golden boon of soul, found not, alas!
A pilgrim to all shrines, a worshiper
At none, I turned me toward my home to face
My fate and beg the love and hand of her

I dared not claim through any worthy faith,
Yet deemed that stay, with toil and student's lore,
The last that held me hope—

      "Hermit, what saith
 The feeble pulse? The fitful dream is o'er,
The time is short; it boots thee not to know
 The rest, to hold a withered spray of life
In thy strong hands. I die, but quickly go,
Ere thou hast laid me in a grave below
 Your mountain pine, and seek, if still in life,
 This sad-browed maid, this second soul of mine."
Then from his hand he drew a golden band,
 Studded with one rich stone, and held it forth.
"Take this; she will recall and understand
 The message that it bears, and deem it worth
All riches of Golconda's store—the last
 Of all her gifts, when that she dare not give,
Through deep-wrought fear, herself into my arms,
 And held me to return, when hope should live
In equal purpose with my wish. It charms
 That hope from death, and, like the Levite's gems,
Burns strangely bright, since heaven no more condemns.

"Nine leagues to westward, by the south, unless
 My judgment errs, the city lies, war-scarred
And wasted now by plague. There Madeline,
 An angel to the poor (whose wilderness
 Is lighter for her face), by mercy starred,
Waits with the sick—and she self-same maid

Of whom I spake. To her, if thou shalt find,
   Say that the spoiler's hand at last was staid;
At evening time the morning's glory shined,
   And that I died with faith in Him alone
Who sees the sparrows fall; my soul resigned
   To Him who died. If that sweet blood atone,
My snared and trembling soul shall rest in peace.

"Lo, now is life! a vision sweetly dawns
   Like morning through the dome of forest-trees
Of that old story told by thralldom's tongue
   In those fair days before my shame, which frees
The soul while yet it serves; a tale that wrung
   Compassion from the grave and senseless stones;
But by what law it works these late results,
   And strengthens every noble wish to live,
I know not, but 'tis so. I feel the pulse
   Of ampler thought and warmer hope relieve
The dull, insipid course that reason owns.
   How should a slave know this and not my sire,
Gifted with mind to shame a golden age?
   How reached my soul aphelion of desire
To read faith's mystery-lighted page?"

The lids dropped on the sunken eyes; the breast
   Was still, yet moved, anon, the pallid lips.
"At even time," they faintly said, "light—rest!
   At even time, at even time!" As slips
A star behind the gloom of midnight clouds,
   The spirit seemed to slip into the realm

Of shades, leaving the hermit in his moods,
  Rocking of spirit worlds, as in a dream.

All day he toiled, till eve, to make a grave,
  And when the stars shone brightly forth above,
Not turning toward the death-kept couch, and save
  To break his day-long fast, staid not through love
Of him now dead and her who loved too well.
  So all night long by Bear and Dipper's aid
He journeyed westward by the south.   Through fell
  And gorge, by farm and lonely cot, he made
His swerveless way.   The watch-dog's midnight bark,
  The owlet's hoot or snort of startled hind,
  Were all the sounds he heard, save that the wind
With thin and bated voice breathed through the dark
  Roofed pines and died in soughings far away.
At length there came a sound of passing waves,
  Of distant waters moaning on their way;
  Then o'er the forest broke the gloaming day,
And soon the city's spires against the sky
  Rose dark and tall, and in the misty light
He saw he walked a lovely garden.   High
  The white-stemmed poplars rose, and left and right
Were fragrant flowers, green vines; and marble shapes
  Cold white as winter's wing, thereby he knew
His feet were once more with the dreamless dead.
Now sepultures, with clods still damp and red,
  Unmarked, undecked, by fives, by tens, and scores,
Opposed each marble shape.   Cold, dripping dew,
  The tears that mourning darkness kindly pours

9

From starry eyes upon the smitten earth,
Gemmed every leaf, as though she knew
  Man's special woe and wept with deeper grief.
Weary the hermit sat him down, and drew
  His hermit cloak about his form and read
The names upon the nearest stones.   Dim through
  The vine-foiled windows 'twixt the myrtle shade
And wide magnolia-boughs, the river's glint
  Rose to his sight.   A· drawing back, a dread
To face his fellows, e'en to the point
  Of wavering faith, opposed his promise made.

The mist-dispelling sun now waking, drew
  His chariot's golden wheel above the flood
And scattered amber light, that on the dew
  Wrought rainbow beauty through the waking wood,
Where glory called to glory.   Solemn sounds
  Of distant bells disturbed the hermit's ears
And woke from out his memory's still profounds
  Deep thoughts that sweetened hope in other years.
He rose and moved with quick, impatient pace
Along the bordered path, fixing his gaze
  Upon the distant tower whence came those peals
That pleased and gloomed his soul at once.   Not wide
  He wandered from his seat, with fears and ills
Of soul forgotten, when he saw beside
  The path, deep in the drooping willow's shade,
And hidden half by lowly daffodils
  And autumn-penciled grass, a grave new made,

O'er which but once had brooded sable night:
    A broken lily at its head, a spray
Of cypress by its side, spoke of the blight
    That closed untimely some young spirit's day.
A sudden pallor swept the hermit's face,
    And consternation checked his cheerful mien—
What if the rude white cross that marked the place
    Fulfilled his fears with tale of Madeline?

Soon had his eyes the doubtful story read;
    But now the monkish sexton, like a ghost,
Glided from out the shade with silent tread
    And stood within the hermit's sight. As lost
To reason, each gazed on the other's face,
    Moveless and speechless for a time. At last
The hermit spake, full anxious to displace
    The burden from his mind: "O ancient man,
I come from far with tidings for a maid
    Of one whose life is fled; but fate outran,
I deem, my steps. Fear tells me here is laid
    That Madeline whom all the city blessed;
If so it prove, thou need'st not know the rest."

"I wist not if she live this morn, yet know
    She lies not here, nor had been laid, at eve,
In any grave; for with the dying glow
    Of yester sun, word came that she did live,
And if her strength endured till dawn again,
    She would survive; but yon loud death-bell's tones,
That woke me from disturbèd sleep, sustain

The doubt I held, for scarce its lips with moans
So deep had knolled another's journey hence."

"It fits me not, O sire," the hermit cried,
    "To walk through peopled streets again, and since
It more than seems she liveth not, should pride
    Of literal faith impel me to attaint
A vow so long observed?   Take this," and forth
    He drew the student's ring, "take this; acquaint
The maid, if still in life, of this my tale.
    The place is thrice three leagues to east, by north;
A ragged hill that stands above the vale
    Where westward turns the tide of dark Yazoo;
A hermit's cot beside a runlet's wave;
    A lonely pine, piercing th' eternal blue,
That weeps above her lover's unfilled grave,
    Will hold for many a mile the traveler's view."

This said, the hermit slowly turned and strode
With steady pace adown the silent wood.

CANTO EIGHTH.

I.

HAIL! living Christ, whose soul hath borne the weight,
The mountain weight, of all our human guilt;
Whose voice was poured through dark-leaved Olivet
In one wild prayer for strength to die; who spilt
Thy princely blood—blood without taint of guilt—
Long lineaged blood and older than the sun,
Or any star, or angel pulse that hilt
Of wrathful sword had warmed ere was begun
That crystal wonder con-told to wide renown.

First bloom of past eternity! thy love
Still fruits and blossoms in the vernal glow
Of these our fateful years. The forms that move
In legioned myriads, shadowy, slow,
Into the death-marged realms of silence, go
Heeded of love alive forevermore.
While hanging in the shades of that last woe
Wrought in Golgotha's place, thy soul's eye bore,
Clear imaged, all—from, face and heart to burning core.

Risen, alive! all hail! mild as the light
Of the young day that treads o'er violets,
Earliest blown of forms that earth bedight;

Yet awful as the thunder-flame that jets
From heaven's storm-parted lips when wrath begets
   A judgment speech! I clothe me in that first,
Lifted from winter death, like violets,
   But from that last, when like a sword it thirst,
Hide me, gray cross—hide me from that last lightning
     burst!

Loud speaks a voice whose sacred accents say,
   Or seem: "O lowly taught, thou canst not see
What wonders crowd thy path, by night, by day;
   How near unnumbered hosts encompass thee,
What throbbing chords thou daily treadest on
   That wake in discord or in harmony;
Thy searching sight meets here its horizon,
   But yon blue heights thy newborn thoughts shall
     tread,
With suns for stepping-stones, till glory crown thy head!"

II.

The day's red orb dropped through the quivering haze
   That wrapped the marge of Yazoo's cypress glades,
While long slant splendors wrought their golden maze
   From mount to stream, and bridged the abyss of shades
Adown which fell the white-robed thistle mote,
   Blown from the copses of the hills.   Echo
Woke all her genii from their caves and caught
   The rising harmonies, and far below
And high above the listening crags, each fraught
   With elfin changes, threw them note by note.

With crown of sweat about his brow, and feet
 Grown sore and weary in the day-long toil,
Into his wild the hermit made retreat;
 Slowly he climbed the shadowy slope, and, while
In one wide curtain from the orbless sky
 The silver twilight hung, passed o'er the stile
And to his cot.

     Is knowledge what we deem,
Or what our skeptic souls would give it name?
 Is there no over-soul to tell us when we dream,
If dream we true or false? There bides to claim
 Our feal to law, and smites if heeded not,
Conscience, so called for lack of better word;
 But consciousness is ampler, unbegot,
Begetting every child of sense and thought;
 May not it, then, some time, somehow, have heard
Unlawful things, laying a feeble ear
 Against the walls of God's great secret house?
One law is regnant, binding far and near
 The parts of this wide whole, the universe,
Into a kinship of desires that rouse
 A universal thought, and so its course
Must sometimes glow with unspent thoughts of God
 While through the lowliest heart it burns.

       A calm
Foreboding of delight, while yet he trod
 The pillared woods, grew in the hermit's mind;
The eager air seemed laden with the balm
 And spices of a rifled tomb, and, swift and kind,

Disparted souls seemed moving toward their rest.

  A pulse of angel pinions rustling nigh,

Of angel breathings low, his soul confessed

  As to the cot he passed; yet mortal eye,

Since at the lonely tomb of Bethany

  The Son of Mary stood, was never smote

With wonder like the hermit's owned. Lo! there

  The death couch stood, but all unwrought

The tale it lately told. Smoothed down with care,

  The rustic robes were o'er the grass mat spread;

The water cruise stood emptied of its draught;

  The chair on which the garments of the dead

At eve before had lain now owned to naught

  Save the torn scarf that girt his loins at death.

A foot-print on the wind-dashed fallow pressed,

  And fellowed in the sand and sumac heath

That balked the runlet's course, told how his guest,

  Reviving, passed into the waste again;

And so the hermit moved him to and fro

  Between the cot and unfilled grave, still fain

To find a clew to something less than marvel's awe.

Meantime into a sylvan space, a lawn

  Of nature planned, above which burned the flame

Of autumn leaves, at point five leagues removed

  From the smit city, slowly moving, came

The low wheels of a *diligence*. The hands

  That reined the lagging jades trembled with age,

A gray-haired Ethiop's—prince of mangrove lands

On the dark coast; proved in long bondage,
Now free, but held by stronger bond as hers
  Who sate, pale-faced and weary, in the coach:
In like he served through all her maiden years
  The mother till a bride, then bound, in such
Till death; therefrom the daughter, faithful still.
Now halting, from the clear wave of a rill
  He raised a full cup to the pale lips' touch
And stood, with head made bare, waiting his lady's will.

Drink, pale-lipped Madeline, the heaven-pledged cup!
  God brewed it in the summer cloud and stored
Deep in the summer caves, whence unto hope
  A full libation naiads' hands have poured
From lily urns its coolness forth; no dregs
  Are in its depths, for lo! is passed for aye
Thy bitter cup. No more thy spirit begs
  In vain a joyous boon. Drink to the day
Of happy love—the day that was—that is!
Two wonders in the earth beneath are seen,
  Transcending all—a soul that keeps its bliss
Through stainless faith and one that finds again
  Its bliss through purifying love. Drink deep,
O stainless maid; drink to the purified,
  The chastened one, whose shining feet now keep
Glad movement, hasting swiftly to thy side;
  He lives whose soul is brother unto thine!
The fallen leaves betray his coming steps;
  The leaves above, with accents half divine,
Repeat his name. "He lives; he comes; he leaps,"

They cry.   Receive thine exile into rest.
A sudden start; a maiden's fitful cry;
  Eyes turned to eyes, and pale lips unto pale lips pressed.
Too long the care, too great the ecstasy
Of hope revived—swoon, gentle heart, not die!
  'Tis well, 'tis well; thyself shalt wake to rest!

Like the slow tide of tropic streams deep steeped
  In the warm odors of the falling molds
Of thousand drooping boughs, eve onward crept,
  Balm sweetened, toward the west.   The primrose folds
Its waxen leaves to ope again when dies
  The regal sun in twilight's holy shade.
So oped the folded lids of love-blessed eyes
  That might not drink its brightness wonder rayed.

" Back from the dead," the white lips breathed, when first
  They caught the vital air, " back from the dead
Thou art returned to me.   What power has burst
  Thy double bond, for free my soul doth read
Thou art—alive and free, thrice free ? "   They spake
  Glad-voiced, when he, the youth, speechless till then,
Replied: " Yea, back from more than dead; awake
  To more than life—to light, to liberty
Of those high thoughts we early proved; made such
  Through knowledge of that Christ by whom I stand,
And shall through future days, till magic touch
  Of the arch-seraphim Ithuriel's wand
Shall lift me to the height of his tall form.

Thou hast done well that thou didst come.   Our feet
Are not misled, I deem, if faith conform
  To His fair will who did our faith beget,
And yet so late I read that will; the peace
  Therefrom so new, perchance I do construe
Somewhat above that it may bind or please;
  Howbeit, hence it led me on, and true
I find my hope that thou art still in life,
  And that the old-time warmth abides within
The twilight circle of thine eyes.   Joy rife,
  A thousand passion fires within me burn
And visions of the sunny years to be;
  But summer waits till winter's soul expires,
So to a tale of wand'rings list and learn
  Whence rose my sin-scathed soul to light and lease
Of nobler walk.
                    "How long, or by what chance
I wandered in the hoary wild, ere ease
  Of pain, or thought's clear vision broke the trance
Of mind, I may not say; all misty is
  From day thy tender eyes looked on me ill
Till yester dawn. 'Twas then I knew surprise,
  And fear o'ertook my soul.   I woke with still
A thought that thou wert nigh; but other eyes
  Regarded me: a hermit to his cot
Had borne me, and with brother's tenderness
  Had watched my malady, that seemed begot
Of death, and death seemed close and hard to press
  The bated life, until he deemed I died

And laid his finger tips upon my lids
  In office kind. Deep peace was multiplied
That hour within; for all that morn, as hides
  The feathered waif when storms are loud, my soul
Had hid in prayer; and voices of the days
  We love, blown from the aspen-shaded knoll
Held by the brown-roofed chapel, where to praise
  And worship oft our childish feet were led,
Came memory sweet upon my ear. I knew
  I lived, or deemed it so, yet for the dead
Was marked, and pulse and sentient life withdrew
  And hid them in the inner heart.

                    " Slow paced,
The hermit passed into the day, then reigned
  A tomb-like silence; thence no more I traced
The course of sense : a vision's light obtained
  Assent and clothed, like woven flame, my brain.
Dreams have I known, in sleep, that led afar
  Through changes of the hidden world and pain
Or joy sustained, but never such fair star
  Of trance or fancy led my sight. To rise
I seemed, leaving my grosser part still prone
  Upon the hermit's couch, yet everywise
Perfect the part that stood and passed alone
Into a coast-land fringed with orange-groves,
And goodly fair to look upon ; a glow
Of ebbing day, like that which now expires,
Lent holy silence to the hour. My steps

Bent slowly downward to the sea that lapped
With summer drowsiness the pebbly beach.
I strained my eyes and heart to read a sign,
A token of the over-soul that walks
Through summer seas or breathes imperial strength
Reclining midst the mountain shades.   One sail
Whose pennant pointed toward the Isthmic coast,
Through dark Campeachy's darker waste, was all
The blue veil's misty folds allowed my sight;
Glowed not the light of eld that floated down
The zodiacal paths into my soul,
When in my own thy hand was pressed, now cold,
I thought, beneath the upland's thymy sod.
Thereat I hated life and feared the death
I could not die.   Through unfrequented ways
I turned and climbed a wooded steep, hard by
A soft-voiced stream that dropped, full-waved and clear,
Into the deep *Nirvana* of the bay.
Great oaks, moss-grown and century gnarled, rose high,
And clasped in rugged arms, as lovers might
Their circlet-plighted maids, magnolia-trees,
Decked in the white wealth of their bridal pride.
I had not thought since time began that foot,
Save mine, had pressed that virgin mold; an air
Of the divine was there; a censer smell
Of woodland sacrifice and worship filled
The balmy lapses of the tangled shade;
In the wood's deep heart, half hid by drooping vines
Pendant from one dark-fronded ash that stood

Taller than all his kind, I came upon
A lonely mound and sate me down in thought.

" Darkness was near full and still descending night
Her pall spread over heaven,. till, like a soul
Let loose from clay, the moon leaped on the sea
And poured its light through all the woven gloom
Of vines and odorous boughs that shut me in.
Clothed in the moonlight's splendor, one came forth
From out the vine-screened depths, and, standing near,
Made low obeisance and began to speak:
' Fair greetings, son ! long have I waited here
The coming of thy steps.'   With this I looked
More closely on his form.   His flowing hair,
White as the frost on Sitkan hills, fell full
Upon his shoulders bare, athwart which hung
A silken badge, with tinsel emblems set.
His swarthy face was crossed by many a line
That age, not care, had wrought. .

                                   "After a pause,
And stretching forth his hand, he thus went on :
' My words are dark; but know I am the last
Of a long line of priestly men who stood
Within the shrines of that Atlantic Isle
Long perished, but renowned in all the earth.
All wisdom of all times, Indic, Egyptic,
Iranic and the roots of the fair tree
Etruscan grown, concentered in that school
Of wisest fellowship, and sense of things

That, like the leaf, lie folded in the years
Of dark futurity. At night—the last
Of all her history, wherein to rise no more
The fair isle sank into the hungry seas—
A remnant of the holy house embarked
And, heaven led, pitched on these shores and built
Great mounds and many a sinuous temple wall,
In ruins long—I, the latest and alone,
Have sat me here a hundred circling years,
Poring the rolls of Ayar-manco-topa,
Sage of mighty soul. Therein 'tis writ
That he who keeps the holy line alone
Shall bide him in this vine-embowered place
And forth conduct whoever sits him first
Upon this grassy bosk—if so he will—
Unto an isle far in the summer sea,
Where leaps to kiss of living light the spray
Of the clear Fount of Youth, whereof who drinks
Forgets his present pain and evermore
Shall know his early dreams, and strength
Wherewith to compass hope. And thou art first.

" Instant,"I cried, with wildness in my voice
' Lead forth, O holy man, to that fair isle!
Surely the gods are wise and kind, and fate
Forgets its evil end! I follow thee
To that new hope, as one of blindness smit
Follows the guiding hand through dangerous paths.'
Few steps brought to the stream's green banks our feet;

And there, fast moored, beneath a rock that dripped
With tinkling water drops, a white-winged boat,
Made ready for the wave.   Quickly embarked,
The moorings loosed, we pointed toward the deep.
The land-breeze fed the trembling sails, and soon
The keel leaped to the white arms of the surf,
And sang a listless song of one soft note.
The breeze rose to a gale—a gale from skies
Of cloudless blue, o'erflecked with isles of fire.
Behind the rattling sails and groaning spars
The prophet sate to helm the bark and sang,
Or chanted loud, a hymn of ancient lore.
All wisdom of all times pulsed through its words,
And hope of future days—not earth's, I ween.
Much more he sang, but this mine ears retained:

SONG.

1 "'Man clings to time! the ebbing tide sweeps out,
      Leaving a beach of trodden sands behind,
   Fringed with a range of hoary shades that flout
      Funereal banners in the sobbing wind;
   And ghostly shapes walk in the dim inane,
      Dumb with the draught of Lethe's slumb'rous wave,
   Or lade the denser gloom with rueful plain,
      While dull Oblivion smiles to hear them rave.

2 "'Beyond that strip of coast-line trodden bare,
      Beyond the long gray swell of tossing gloom,
   Cinctured with fading sunlight here and there,
      Few know the secrets of that realm of doom;

Few souls have pierced beyond its middle wild,
   Still fewer heard the pulsing ocean beat
In languid measures on the rocks up-piled,
   Its other shore, bereft of light and heat.

3 " ' Some, passing thence, returned with thrilling tale
   Of what opposed their sight the journey on,
Of marble wonders fallen low, with trail
   Of ruin everywhere; of beauty gone
From palaces and courts of mighty kings.
   Where fell the splendor of a thousand years
Now falls the night of waste, and ivy clings
   To shrines once boasting royal worshipers.

4 " ' We cling to life! the ebbing tide sweeps out;
   A leaden sky infolds the foaming deep;
Faint Occidental flushes dance about
   The far horizon, where the billows keep
Their wavering line opposed against its blue;
   A zodiacal gloam sifts through the haze
And timeward falls, with weird and wasted hue;
   Dies on the strand or on the distant maze.

5 " ' These be the tokens of a sunken sun
   And of the fading day, whose orbèd rays,
Paling from narrower skies, have but begun
   To weave the woofèd splendors of the days
Immortal named.   Yet still we cling to life,
   And cast the anchor, moved by doubt's alarm
To hear the ocean break in fitful strife
   Or see the night-racks fly before the storm!
  10

6 " ' Dank are the landward shades and wet with dew
    The feathery fronds, outlined against the mist,
Whose leaden zone gains surely on the view.
    Launch forth into the deep, though fears resist!
The Happy Isles and Lotus Coasts are hid
    Far in the watery wastes. Launch forth to peace!
The sun-dyed clouds foretype thy joy and bid
    As Argonauts to seek the Golden Fleece!'

"The bark swept on before the sleepless wind
    And slipped, at morn, into a waste of reefs
Green with the coral palm and ivies twined
    About the tropic beach; tall reeds and sheafs
Of lush green grass whispered above the sea.
    Fair-plumaged birds battled with burnished wings
The warm-breathed gale, and all things glad and free
    Told of a summer in whose fullness springs
All rapture of delight that, passing into song,
    To thralldom charms the list'ning soul. The day
Had faded half and, falling deep among
    The lessening banks, the winds had died away;
But in a current of the sea the boat
    Was drifting toward a mist-veiled coast with hue
Of purpling light beyond. As bubbles float
    Upon the stream, we floated on and drew.
    Our course hard on a rocky cove and threw
The anchor by the shore. The sinking sun
    Stretched forth his beamy hands and held the mist
High o'er the Happy Isle, when brightly shone

Its nameless beauty on our sight.   I kissed
The mossy rocks and left my feeble lips
   Buried a moment in the cooling dew,
   When lo ! a sound of gurgling water drew
My fancy toward the inner isle.   My heart
   Beat like a hunted stag's; hope burned anew
In every breath : waters of youth that part
   The soul from all its evil fears flowed near.
Led by the priest, soon to the welling wave
   I came and stood, feasting desire.   Light clear,
And deep as heaven's blue well, it seemed and gave
   Reflected wonders from its depths.   I stooped
To drink, but ere my lips had touched the wave
   It shrank and died, and moistless sand instead
Filled the deep cave.   I rose, and all the isle
   Was changed into a waste of sand that spread
From shore to shore ; nor sign of life the while,
   Nor sound of living thing, save the dark priest,
   And he, a shadow grown, faded to mist
And passed, like all my hopes, away.   A voice
   Came with the last faint trace of shade that told
The outline of his form : 'Hollow the noise
   Of human pride and wisdom late or old ;
Death is the tree and death must be the fruit.'

" Prone to the earth I fell and laid in dust
   The lips deceived and cried, 'Above the brute
No whit is man; nobler in form, with trust
   In higher things, but both go downward to the earth.'

The heart within me died, and seemed to blend
    With parent clay, resolved to primal birth;
But since, in death or kind relief, must end
    Our bitterest woe, I waited, hoping naught,
When one with burning finger smote my cheek;
    Whereat I rose, and lo! a change was wrought
In all the isle, that seemed no isle, nor bleak
    And waste, but a most sacred land and strewed,
Toward every wind of heaven, with wonders wide;
    Its vales and terraced hills, of old, to tread
And the swift toil of thousands woke with pride
    Of fruitful years; but now no mortal fares,
Or shall fare, through forever. The wild palm
    In leagues of vacancy hails the soft airs
That breathe a scent of terebinth and balm
    Over the dust of many a ruined pile
That swells from the smooth stretch of goodly plains,
    Or keeps the stately shape and dim profile
Of ancient grandeur, slowly wrought in reigns
    Of peaceful kings. There was nor voice nor sound
What time I stood with fate contending there,
    But pain was grown to stark despair and bound
With rueless chains.
                    "Lo! where with aimless stare
    I gazed, a mount sloped upward toward the skies
Against which stood a cross, and round it played
    A mystic light, fanned to a glow by sighs
That angels breathed—sighs of desire, not made
    Of grief.

" Down from the mount a Form moved slow,
Until it stood and looked upon my face;
   Benignly calm it gazed and spake in low
And measured tones: 'Arise, thou fallen soul; grace
   Bids thee rise. Thy will has died, but lives; I
Who speak, the living Christ, shall make thee stand.
   I am thy strength unto eternity.'

" I seemed to quaff a cup held in a hand
   To me invisible : a cup I knew—
I could but know the truth—that kings and seers
   And mighty ones of old had quaffed. The dew
Distilled in Paradise and sweetened airs
   Blown from its hills across the lily marge
Of life's clear wave had not more grateful proved
   To my faint soul. What owned I then ? Deep, large,
And calm as ether's sea, heaven's fullness moved
   Upon my sense, and moved with every draught.
O holy cup ! O very grail ! I drank
   And, drinking, felt within me power and craft
Of evil motions die. Not then a blank,
   As I had prayed a time before, my life
Of darker thoughts and appetite, but force
   And argument sustaining trust : a strife
With doubt, and ever so to be.

               " What course
The spirit's currents ran was changed. The note
   Discordant in our harmony of love
Was drowned in faith's full-measured song. I wote

That man is spirit more than flesh : I strove,
Therefore, no more, and mind o'er flesh was staid.
   I knew the kingly words of Him whose hands,
Once pierced, sustained the universe. He laid
   On me (O awful joy!) those kingly hands,
And all His soul passed into mine. I made
   Thereat to rise, spurning the desert's sands,
But woke that moment in the hermit's cot ;
   And all is well! Ah! do we sit this hour
In Paradise? and is thy face unwrought
   Of earthly hue, and angel's made, that power
Of beauty soul-consuming it reveals?
   Afar in joyless paths I vainly sought
To find what this good hour my bosom fills :
   I wake from trance of morbid fear to thought
Of those fair days wherein our wedded souls
   Shall walk to triumph of their early dream,
   And lo! our token: fades the twilight's bolder gleam,
But in his own clear light the Star of Evening rolls ! "

L'ENVOI.

The fortnight of my tale is done; I seal
This Book of Life and, sealing, steal
Into that silence whence I came. He cares
Who smote these strings vibrant to many airs,
He cares but little for the fleeting praise
That lives on transient lips. He sought to raise
A beacon by a storm-swept coast. If there
Some sin-tossed soul shall see and fare
   To hope and God, he is repaid.

                        My ears
Approve a sound of myriad feet; the years
That are to be reverberate with song
And pæan shout of conquering hosts that throng
The fields of strife and, thronging, turn the tide
Toward victory's perfect day.   Faith, Hope abide,
And Love; and, led by Him, the living Form,
I send this arrow at the Python worm.

THE END.